8/17

Leading a Family Business

Leading a Family Business

Best Practices for Long-Term Stewardship

Justin B. Craig, PhD, and Ken Moores, PhD

PRAEGER ™

An Imprint of ABC-CLIO, LLC
Santa Barbara, California • Denver, Colorado

Library of Congress Cataloging-in-Publication Data

Names: Craig, Justin B., author. | Moores, Ken, author.
Title: Leading a family business : best practices for long-term stewardship /
    Justin B. Craig, PhD, and Ken Moores, PhD.
Description: Santa Barbara, California : Praeger, [2017] | Includes bibliographical
    references and index.
Identifiers: LCCN 2017010648 (print) | LCCN 2017023708 (ebook) |
    ISBN 9781440855337 (ebook) | ISBN 9781440855320 (alk. paper)
Subjects: LCSH: Family-owned business enterprises.
Classification: LCC HD62.25 (ebook) | LCC HD62.25 .C73 2017 (print) |
    DDC 658.4/092—dc23
LC record available at https://lccn.loc.gov/2017010648

ISBN: 978-1-4408-5532-0
EISBN: 978-1-4408-5533-7

21 20 19 18 17   1 2 3 4 5

This book is also available as an eBook.

Praeger
An Imprint of ABC-CLIO, LLC

ABC-CLIO, LLC
130 Cremona Drive, P.O. Box 1911
Santa Barbara, California 93116-1911
www.abc-clio.com

This book is printed on acid-free paper ∞

Manufactured in the United States of America

Contents

White Board Illustrations

Tables and Diagrams

Tables

Diagrams

Exemplar Stories

Chapter 2: Architecture

Case Study: John L. Ward and Canh Tran, *Generational Transition and Transformation,* unpublished case, Kellogg School of Management, 2006.

Chapter 3: Governance

Case Study: John Ward and Canh Tran, *Scott Family Enterprises (A): Defining Fair Process for Cousin Owners,* Kellogg Case #5-204-267(A), published 2004.

Chapter 4: Entrepreneurship

Case Study: John Ward and Elly Andriopoulou, *The Oberman Family and Omeda Communications Inc.,* Kellogg Case #5-105-003, published 2006.

Chapter 5: Stewardship

Case Study: John Ward, Brent C. Stern, Carol Adler Zsolnay, and Sachin Waikar, *ATF, Inc.: Fasteners and Family,* Kellogg Case #5-113-004, published 2016.

Chapter 7: The Steward

Case Study: John Ward, Carol Adler Zsolnay, and Sachin Waikar, *How to Motivate the Fifth Generation? Balancing Engagement and Entitlement at Lee Kum Kee,* Kellogg Case #5-214-251, published 2016.

Chapter 8: The Architect

Case Study: John Ward and Carol Adler Zsolnay, *The Murugappa Group: Centuries-Old Business Heritage and Tradition*, Kellogg Case #5-104-011, published 2004.

Chapter 9: The Governor

Case Study: John Ward, Carol Adler Zsolnay, and Sachin Waikar, *A Diamond in the Rough: J.M. Huber and the PATH Business*, Kellogg Case #5-416-757, published 2017.

Chapter 10: The Entrepreneur

Case Study: Lloyd Shefsky and Carol Adler Zsolnay, *Abt Electronics: Next Steps in a Parent/Sibling-Managed Family Business*, Kellogg Case #5-210-258, published 2010.

Preface

This book is a business narrative. A story. Therefore, it is different from the books you would typically find on this topic. It is not a textbook, not a biography, and certainly not a how-to solutions-focused panacea. It does not contain checklists or other instruments. Instead, it is focused on helping you to develop your thinking (and thinking skills) about family business leadership and its key differences from other types of businesses.

The story we tell is firmly grounded in rigorous research, that of ours and others. We consider that research a form of storytelling. But the trouble with most research is that those who need to read it don't, and those who don't need to read it do, and often miss the point that the storyteller/researcher is making. Therefore, understanding this, we thought the best way to bring meaningful research to those who need it most is to tell the story of the emergent body of family business research in a way that would entice readership.

The main character in our story is Stewart Macduff, a third-generation family business leader. His circumstances are couched in a learning journey that sees him interpreting experiences and observations to build capacity to lead both his family and his business. Throughout, we include theory-driven evidenced-based frameworks to help tell his story.

We acknowledge the many researcher storytellers who have helped us create this character and his story and include references to some, but certainly not all, of the research that has helped us on our own learning journey.

We also acknowledge the countless business families across the world who have generously shared, and continue to share, their stories in order to help researchers like us to craft our stories, as it is only from their stories that we can develop knowledge and understanding of their world. It is how we learn. They are our teachers.

Finally, we sincerely thank those who have helped make this storytelling project possible. A more committed team is hard to imagine.

Justin and Ken

CHAPTER ONE

Introducing Stewart Macduff

Everything that every successful effective manager does is sandwiched between action on the ground and reflection in the abstract. Action without refection is thoughtless; reflection without action is passive. Every manager has to find a way to combine these two mindsets—to function at the point where reflective thinking meets practical doing.

—Jonathan Gosling and Henry Mintzberg (2003)

My name is Stewart Macduff. I lead a family business. A sometimes lonely task. What follows is a collection of reflections and insights, mine and others, which I feel compelled to share because my experience is that leading a family business comes with limited instructions. In fact, I compare my role as a leader of a multigenerational family business as being a lot like struggling with "flat-pack" furniture, which looks great in the showroom but it is a completely different story when you try to piece it all together, with (very) limited useful instructions and nothing but an "Allen" key.

And though my office and home bookshelves are replete with leadership books from the most respected thinkers, and my walls are covered with all sorts of academic qualifications and objects of attainment that suggest I know what I am doing, the reality is that I continue to be challenged every single day. Actually, *multiple times* every single day.

I have now completed the best part of 10 years in this leadership role, and my reflections about these challenges outlined here are aimed at distilling the wisdom of our ways for subsequent generations. I reentered the business after a successful professional career outside, at the request of my second-generation leader father, and was fortunate to learn some aspects of our uniqueness directly from him. Following an extended apprenticeship, I eventually assumed leadership of the business.

Put simply, leading a family business is both the most rewarding and challenging job on the planet. A job that is shared by so many of us from around the world given that as a class of business our family firms numerically dominate all free enterprise economies. But our rewards and challenges in these leadership roles are fundamentally different from those of our colleagues who lead widely held corporations.

The motivation behind this book is very consistent with the notion that a characteristic of family businesses is that they (i.e., we) pursue unconventional strategies. Thus, as I pondered writing this book, I came to the conclusion that, in order to be of any real benefit to the family business community, what is required is not another conventional "how to" management or leadership publication. Rather, and this is what I endeavor to deliver, this is a book that reflects my (our) everyday life while being also firmly grounded in robust and defendable frameworks. This everyday life to which I refer is not about either/or decisions. It is a both/and world family business leaders occupy as we juggle commitments to both the business and the family. Yes, somewhat paradoxical. But, as will soon become evident, the approach I pursue is intentionally paradoxical because if there is one thing that I know about my world, it is that it is paradox central. And paradoxes can't be solved, only managed. Therefore, consider this time well spent in *Paradox School*.

The frameworks I introduce throughout the chapters that follow are tested in my time-honored "white board thinking" approach to leadership. Importantly, they are what I like to describe as "digestible" and, even more poignantly, as "able to be replicated on a napkin or drink coaster." While that may sound trite, it is actually important to note. My experience is that, often, I need to communicate my "philosophies of leadership" (let's call them that) in nontraditional educational settings and usually I am within an arm's length of a napkin or a drink coaster. Think family wedding when seated with a cousin not working in the business and with whom you never get one-on-one time; think family birthday celebration with extended family when a niece is "suddenly" interested in the mechanics of the business; think after-work drinks with nonfamily executives who are curious to better understand how the family and ownership systems interface with their roles in management, for example. Therefore, translating my "white board frames" to be as efficient and effective as possible needs to also be transportable.

This framing not only raises awareness of fundamental family business issues but also provides hope to tackle the sometimes-overwhelming challenges associated with governance, leadership, management, financial, and interpersonal issues that confront family business leaders. In my experience, the mastery of a distinctive, but simple, language facilitates efficient conversations that assist in developing shared understanding and facilitating collective problem-solving.

Therefore, fundamentally, this book is a leadership roadmap for those in or expecting to take on a leadership role in a family business. But it is more than that. It is also a creative capture of the nuances that face anyone in the family business community. Advisors, financiers, customers, and suppliers as well as family members not involved in the business but who are, or will be, owners will benefit from better understanding why leading a family business is different. Very different.

One thing that I have learned on my pilgrimage to the leader's chair is that context matters. This is important to understand and to remember as you turn the pages and digest the content that I include. The best way to capture this is to remember that all family businesses are the same but different. Another way to say this is the adage they are these days applying to family offices: "If you've seen one family office you've seen . . . one family office." I am of the belief that if you have seen one family business you have seen one family business. However, I am also of the belief that if you adapt a *framework thinking* approach you are able to better understand/appreciate/interpret the nuances of a particular business family (note the subtle but meaningful way I swapped the words "business" and "family").

Therefore, *your* context is *your* context. But keep in mind that this is a movable feast in which the family and the business are in constant flux. Throw the ownership dimension into the mix and you have an ever-evolving context that needs to be managed. I will canvas this in later sections, but, in reality, it is not a dilemma that you are dealing with that tasks you with choosing between the business and the family; it is a series of *trilemmas* in which, for example, you as leader are concurrently dealing with the past, the present, and the future and constantly satisficing family, owners, and managers. Therefore, get used to thinking in threes.

No one said it was easy. Perhaps this is why few to date have taken the deep dive into better understanding why leading a family business is different. I hope my (evidence-based) ramblings shed the light that is needed and which will help you (assuming you are a leader or an aspirant) in your complex *and* rewarding role. My hope is that it will make it marginally less complex and significantly more rewarding. Using the frameworks that I include has certainly been the enlightenment I have required to make my world less complex and also, as a result, has made my role as a business family leader so much more rewarding .and helped me feel less alone.

My Context: The Macduff Family

Though all our circumstances are different, I have found that to better learn from others I need to efficiently understand *their* "family business" world. This way I can understand their perspective. Therefore, let me share my circumstances, briefly, so you can better understand my perspective.

Mine is a third-generation business. Someday, hopefully, a fourth-generation business. My grandfather founded our company at the end of World War II and was able to capitalize on the positivity that engulfed the business world during that time. He was the classic founder who was not really overly focused on planning. Success for him was making a life for his wife and family. In the early days, he measured success by having enough to put food on the table and clothe and educate the kids, of which he had three, two boys and a girl. My dad was the eldest and joined his father in the business after finishing high school. His brother followed two years later but their sister, my aunt, never worked in the business, though her husband did for a while, but let's not go there just yet. Granddad, unfortunately, never saw the business really succeed. He died suddenly at the age of 52, leaving my father in charge at the age of 28. Under my father's stewardship the enterprise grew significantly but not without the usual pains of any growing business. My earliest memories are of my father sharing with my mother how he would struggle to meet payroll or how he was under significant pressure from even the friendliest bankers (for whom he had a not-so-friendly name). I also recall him pontificating about the challenges of having my uncle and aunt as equal partners in the business. Without any formal business education and in the absence of his father acting as a mentor, he succeeded by making decisions he thought in the best interest of all and treating his stakeholders fairly. His style was *old school leadership,* and he really valued relationships, honesty, integrity, and a strong work ethic. It worked for him and for many others in his generation. It is also these values and philosophies that guide our business today.

Things happen in threes in our family, for some reason. I have two siblings, three of us altogether, and each of my father's siblings had three children. Therefore, the sibling partnership that challenged dad has evolved into a cousin consortium made up of three lots of three, that is, nine, not counting spouses. As the eldest in the third generation, this is the family system I now am jointly responsible for, and it is this increasingly complex dynamic that compelled me to find out as much as I could about, and now to be subsequently documenting, the differences between leading a family business and a nonfamily business.

Defining Family Business

Though family businesses are ubiquitous, I have found that there is currently no consensus as to what really constitutes a family business. This remains a contentious issue but one that I am not that interested in pursuing. For me, if challenged to defend how I define family business, I seek safe harbor in the European Union (EU). The EU suggests that to be considered as a family enterprise, a business should meet the following criteria:

- The majority of votes, direct or indirect, is in possession of the founder or those who have acquired the shared capital of the firm or their family members.
- There is at least one representative of the family or kin involved in the management and administration of the firm.

Listed companies can be considered a family enterprise if the family possesses 25 percent of the right to vote mandated by their share capital. The aspect of generational change and the intention to transfer the firm to a family member will also be taken into account. This intention to transfer the firm moves the definition beyond ownership, management, and control components to embrace what is often regarded as the essence of family business—their intended continuity of ownership. It is this notion of continuity that I instill in our family, and it has certainly helped guide our decision making.

The systems theory–inspired Three-Circle Framework (White Board Illustrations 1.1 is named or referred to as "**Three-Circle Framework**") is universally accepted as the best way to describe the differences between family and nonfamily businesses. Simply put, the family firm can be modeled as comprising three overlapping, interacting, and interdependent subsystems of family, managers, and owners. As an open systems model, each subsystem maintains boundaries that separate it from the other subsystems. Each subsystem needs to be governed, but more on that later. This model has been very useful for me in understanding my different roles as a leader. Importantly, it has also helped me understand others' perspectives, depending on the circle or circles they occupy. For example, I now have a role in all three circles. My aunt, who is an owner and a family member (obviously), has a different frame of reference than mine, as she has never worked in the business. Several of my cousins who have never worked in the business and are not yet owners occupy only the family circle. Others have a role in the business but are not yet owners. Having this tool has helped me explain the challenges of family business leadership by better understanding the perspectives of those within the system(s). I recommend you familiarize yourself with the Three-Circle Model and use it to frame your world as I and countless others have.

At the end of most of the chapters in the book I have included a *Trilogy of Lessons for Best Practice Long-Term Stewardship*. Each of the lessons is linked to one of the three circles. I have also included *Recommended Further Reading*, which are books and articles I have found useful in my learning journey, and an *Exemplar Story* that I have collected to illustrate my learnings. Keep the Three Circles top of mind as you read these. It is how I learned.

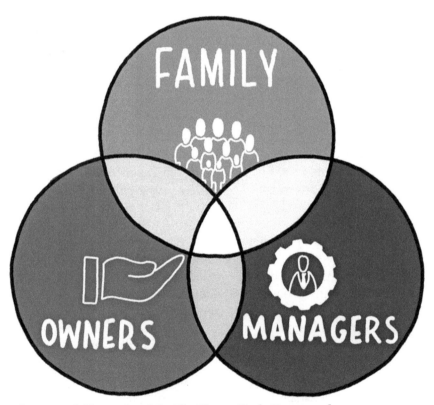

White Board Illustration 1.1. The Three-Circle Framework

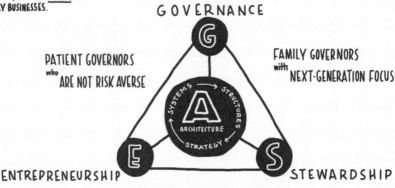

WHERE DIFFERENCES MANIFEST (1) BETWEEN FAMILY and NONFAMILY BUSINESS, and (2) WITHIN FAMILY BUSINESSES.

GOVERNANCE

PATIENT GOVERNORS who ARE NOT RISK AVERSE

FAMILY GOVERNORS with NEXT-GENERATION FOCUS

ENTREPRENEURSHIP

STEWARDSHIP

ENTREPRENEURIAL LONG-TERM-ORIENTED MANAGEMENT and EMPLOYEES

Architecture is HOW we do it.
Governance is the WHO decides WHETHER and WHEN we do it.
Entrepreneurship is the WHAT we do.
Stewardship is the WHY we do it.

White Board Illustration 1.2. The AGES Framework

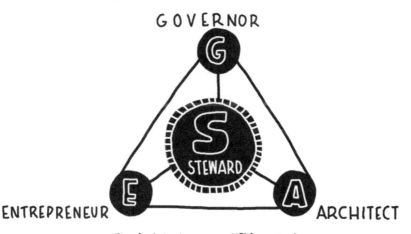

WHERE INDIVIDUAL ROLE DIFFERENCES MANIFEST (1) BETWEEN FAMILY and NONFAMILY BUSINESS, and (2) WITHIN FAMILY BUSINESSES.

GOVERNOR

ENTREPRENEUR

ARCHITECT

The Architect designs HOW we do it.
The Governor decides WHETHER and WHEN we do it.
The Entrepreneur ensures we are innovative at WHAT we do.
The Steward instills WHY we do it.

White Board Illustration 1.3. The SAGE Framework

This Book

I have structured the book into two main sections, each with four subsections. The first half of the book is devoted to the *organizational level* dimensions that distill where differences between family and nonfamily businesses manifest. These dimensions are also useful in understanding where the differences among family businesses arise. Two of the four dimensions (architecture and governance) capture the *structures* that I have come to believe distinguish family businesses. The other two dimensions (entrepreneurship and stewardship) capture the principal *processes* that family business leaders need to master differently than their nonfamily business leader contemporaries.

After zealously studying family businesses and their leaders for a considerable time now I have come to the conclusion that the vastness of the topic can be confusing, even overwhelming. Depending on the definition, most businesses can be defined as family firms. Therefore, to make it simpler for myself, and hopefully others, I needed to develop the framework I introduce to think more efficiently about the field (some refer to it as "the space" or "the genre"). The AGES framework I share is built around the areas in which unique features of family-controlled businesses are evident: their Architecture, Governance, Entrepreneurship, and Stewardship. In broad terms,

1. Architecture includes the underlying observable structures and systems, as well as the origins and outcome differences related to these, that are in place to deliver firm strategy (i.e., the *how*),

2. Governance canvasses both business and family governance structures and some of the processes (i.e., the *who* decides *whether* and *when*),

3. Entrepreneurship covers off strategy and leadership (i.e., the *what*), and

4. Stewardship is arguably the key differentiator that looks at both individual-level and family business–level processes (i.e., the *why*) (White Board Illustration 1.2).

The second half of the book builds off the first but moves the focus from the *organizational* level to the *individual* level. In this section, which is derived from the AGES framework, I will share how I see the four roles that a family business leader needs to concurrently master in order to capably lead both the business and the family. Specifically, introduced as the SAGE framework, he or she needs to be a *Steward*, an *Architect*, a *Governor,* and an *Entrepreneur* (White Board Illustration 1.3).

Throughout I will include insights from leaders (aka the tricks of our trade). I have picked up on what I refer to as my *leadership road less traveled*. I also share case study illustrations and the aforementioned series of *Exemplar Stories,* which are all designed to bring the concepts to life. In addition, I unashamedly borrow from a coterie of professors who have been able to help me make sense of the mess that is the mire that we leaders negotiate every day.

Throughout the chapters I refer to the notion of skillset and mind-set. This applies to almost everything we do in order to achieve any function no matter the circumstance. But in the context of the tasks of a family business leader, I find it a very effective and efficient way to capture what is essentially very complex. The name of the game, as I see it, is for members of the family to be *ready, willing,* and *capable* to contribute to the family and/or business in some capacity, and to do that will require a blend of skillsets and mind-sets. As the business evolves, there is no need for everyone to be pursuing roles for which they are not, nor never will be, appropriately skilled. But to optimally contribute there is a need to adopt a mind-set that is centered on the values and beliefs of the family. Once I (and others in our family) came to terms with that I clarified my roles and responsibilities and, as a consequence, became a better family and business leader.

One last thing to remember: you are not alone.

CHAPTER TWO

Architecture

Values are foundational; change what you do, but not who you are.
This foundation has enabled us to build a strong national brand.
—Jim Ethier, Third-Generation Leader,
Bush Brothers & Company

I want to begin this chapter by raising an important point: *All firms are designed.*

Leaders design and redesign their firms through the structures and systems they put in place to manage their ever-changing, complex worlds. These structures and systems represent a firm's *architecture*—the "A" in the AGES framework here. That's what this chapter is about.

More specifically, architecture captures the structures and systems put in place to deliver a company's strategy (see White Board Illustration 2.1). Therefore, pivotal in the AGES framework, architecture is in place to furnish governance, entrepreneurship, and stewardship (the "G," "E," and "S" of the framework). As you have probably realized from reading this book so far, these dimensions are critical in identifying where differences between family and nonfamily businesses, as well as among family firms, lie. Therefore, let's first examine structures and systems, the dual components of architecture, in more depth. And then I will highlight how a particular strategy, growth, is inextricably linked to the firm's structures and systems and why this differs in our family firm context.

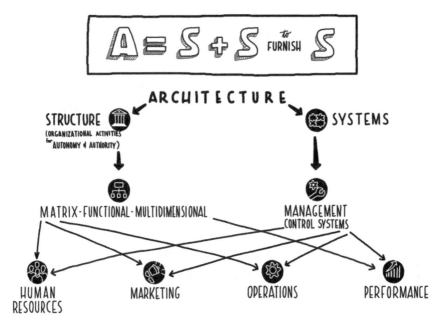

White Board Illustration 2.1. Architecture = Systems and Structures to Deliver Strategy

Structures

Structures frame the organizational design, supporting the processes needed to create order and to carry out organizational tasks. Structures specify the work that needs to be done and how to go about it. To understand the importance of structures, consider the negative consequences when firms pursue a new strategy yet *fail* to review the configuration needed to effectively implement the revised direction. A change in firm strategy typically requires a change in the organizational structure to make it responsive to the "new" needs the reorganization brings about. Fundamentally, structures dictate

1. organizational activities and
2. the authority and autonomy of those individuals or groups designated to undertake these various activities.

Given this, family firms like yours and mine often employ different, sometimes novel, structural options. I have observed a specific pattern when comparing the structures in place with other firms that have a similar pedigree. As our business, like many others, grew first by volume, then by geography, then through vertical or horizontal integration, and finally through product/business diversification, the existing structures lacked the sophistication required to support fully the implementation of what was required for the new stage. As the activities evolved, so did the authority, and autonomy granted to individuals also needs to change.

While I found out the hard way, mostly by trial and error (more the latter), I eventually confirmed that once the company gets to a certain size (when you can't do it all yourself with just a small, dedicated team of all-rounders), there are three basic forms of organizational structure:

1. Functional
2. Multidivisional
3. Matrix

Most small- and medium-sized firms, which would be the background of most reading this, use *functional* structures to divide job responsibilities such as production, accounting, R&D, and human resources. Corporate entities generally operate under a larger umbrella and typically employ *multidivisional* structures. These structures consist of departments that resemble separate businesses or profit centers in which the top corporate officer delegates responsibilities for day-to-day operations and business-unit strategy to division managers. These leaders focus their time on the oversight of managers referred to these days as "Key Reports." In a *matrix* organization, teams are formed in which individuals (Reports) report to two or more managers, usually including a line manager and a staff manager. Matrix structures are highly flexible and readily adaptable to changing circumstances.

Knowing these structural options helps prepare you for change as you move through growth phases. I know many leaders of family businesses whose firms have morphed into large concerns on their watch, and they have, through necessity, adopted multidivisional or matrix structures.

Deciding what structures to implement in your organization depends on a number of factors: the nature of your firm, its size, the environmental conditions under which it operates, and the strategies and activities you are employing to achieve your vision.

Sustainability and continuity require a structure that enables you to make quick decisions in response to market changes. I have observed that, unlike the complex structures nonfamily businesses have, family firms tend to have *flatter* structures. Family firm managers are usually given more power and discretion to make decisions. That creates greater firm agility, enabling managers to take advantage of opportunities that ultimately promote family firm growth and sustainability. There are many ways to create a flatter structure supporting agility, and it's worth pushing the boundaries here. For example, when I told one of my friends we had an "open-door" policy in our organization, he said, "We don't even have office doors. There's no point, as we'd never close them." You get the idea.

I have found that structures that shorten the chain of command and widen the span of managerial control also support greater communication. Typically, job descriptions become broader and task accomplishment relies more on the initiative of the individual employee. This fuzzier definition of authority and responsibilities, however, also generates a paradox, as less formal structures may lead to chaos. A remedy for this is the implementation of better management control systems within the organizational structure.

Therefore, if we assume that family businesses do in fact have in place different structural architectures to support their various activities and that the authority and autonomy granted is a key component of these structures, it is reasonable to suggest that the control systems would also be significantly different. While nonfamily firms are characterized by the sophistication of their management control systems, in order to manage one of their key distinguishing paradoxical advantages of informal formality, the family firm leaders I have observed rely on and promote clan controls—a notion I particularly like and one I think requires no explanation.

Systems

Management control systems include the protocols within firm structures that help deliver the strategy and include, for example, means of dictating how strategic planning is conducted and how other systems are introduced and operationalized idiosyncratically in the firm. Strategic planning systems are perhaps the most important systems an organization can implement. Put simply, a robust strategic planning system enables the firm to formulate strategies and action plans that will help it achieve profitability and sustainability. The strategic planning system helps firm leaders define where they are, where they want to go, and how they will get there. It's pretty simple, really. But there's a proclivity to complicate it.

Some family business leaders, and I was guilty of this, shy away from strategic planning because they think *they* are the central fount of knowledge and thus the sole determiner of direction. That, I found out the hard way, is naïve and self-centered. As I developed as a leader, I realized that planning was indeed my responsibility. The cliché that "failing to plan is planning to fail" is true. How can anyone in your organization function if he or she is unsure of what you want him or her to achieve? Just as real estate experts tout the importance of "location, location, location," so too must family business leaders emphasize "planning, planning, planning."

Performance measures are also part of strategic planning systems and related processes. Performance management systems are essential because these link the organization's goals and strategies to individual and team performance, as a means of increasing organizational effectiveness. Of the many control systems available, I am a fan of Kaplan and Norton's measurement and management tool, the Balanced Scorecard (BSC), as I see it as the most efficient and effective way to emphasize the linkage of measurement to strategy. The BSC has four perspectives:

1. Financial
2. Innovation and learning
3. Customer
4. Internal process

Each of these perspectives can be developed around your family's values and your business vision and mission, in other words, contextualized to develop your own family business scorecard (see White Board Illustration 2.2).

ADAPTED BALANCED SCORECARD FRAMEWORK for FAMILY BUSINESS

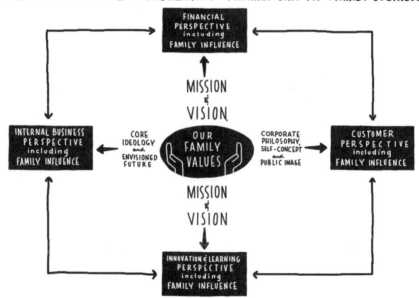

White Board Illustration 2.2. Adapted Balanced Scorecard Framework for Family Business

More specifically, each BSC dimension is individualized by the organization around its vision and mission, and objectives, measures, and targets are established accordingly. The BSC also distinguishes between *lag indicators* and *lead indicators*. For example, financial measures are lag indicators that report on the outcomes of *past* actions. Other lag indicators include return on investment, revenue growth, customer retention costs, new product revenue, and revenue per employee. These lagging outcome indicators need to be complemented (supplemented) by measures of the drivers of *future* financial performance, the so-called lead indicators. Lead indicators are often related to our internal processes and to our innovation and learning, and externally to our customer relationships. Lead indicators include revenue mix, depth of relationships with key stakeholders, customer satisfaction, new product development, diversification preparedness, and contractual arrangements (White Board Illustration 2.3).

Another critical system within family firms that is potentially different in terms of the practices that help them achieve competitive advantage over nonfamily firms has to do with human resource management.

BSC PERSPECTIVE	BUSINESS	FAMILY INFLUENCE
FINANCIAL	▷ REVENUE GROWTH ▷ PRODUCTIVITY IMPROVEMENTS	▷ PREPARE for RETIRING GENERATION ▷ CONSTANT REINVENTION to KEEP FUTURE GENERATIONS INTERESTED in JOINING the BUSINESS
CUSTOMER	▷ OPERATIONAL EXCELLENCE ▷ CUSTOMER INTIMACY ▷ PRODUCT LEADERSHIP	▷ AWARENESS of the FAMILY NAME ▷ USE FAMILY in MARKETING INITIATIVES ▷ QUALITY that REFLECTS FAMILY BRAND IMAGE
INTERNAL PROCESSES	▷ SPURRING INNOVATION ▷ INCREASING CUSTOMER VALUE ▷ ACHIEVING OPERATIONAL EXCELLENCE ▷ PROMOTING CORPORATE CITIZENSHIP	▷ INVESTMENT in TECHNOLOGY that will BENEFIT FUTURE GENERATIONS ▷ PROFESSIONAL WORK PRACTICES that will ATTRACT BEST FAMILY and NONFAMILY EMPLOYEES ▷ PHILANTHROPIC ACTIVITIES
LEARNING & GROWTH	▷ EMPLOYEE CAPABILITIES and SKILLS ▷ TECHNOLOGY ▷ CORPORATE CLIMATE	▷ CREATING CAREER PATHS for FAMILY MEMBERS ▷ MAKING INVOLVEMENT in the BUSINESS a PRIVILEGE ▷ ENCOURAGING and PROVIDING SEED FUNDING for NEW VENTURES PRESENTED by FAMILY MEMBERS

White Board Illustration 2.3. The Balanced Scorecard Perspectives Applied to Business and Family

The strategic management of human resources is important for all businesses, and effective professional human resource management practices (recruitment, selection, compensation, training and development, and appraisal) must be in place, especially for a growing organization. For family firms, it is the hiring process that provides great challenge, especially when it comes to hiring family members. The hiring of family members helps ensure commitment and continuity of the vision of the founding owners. Family members are also likely to feel a stronger sense of responsibility and to take more interest in the company. One of the concerns of family businesses, however, is that the employment of relatives can affect the morale of employees, who may believe that family members, especially if proven inadequate performers, will not get the same treatment as nonfamily employees. This is not typically an issue in nonfamily businesses, by definition.

Moreover, while some families set strict requirements for members who want to join the business, others simply expect the next generation to join after completion of higher education. Best practice suggests that rules or guidelines by which to hire family members should be established and understood by *all* employees in the business. For example, family members who are the future managers of the business should be expected to possess the proficiencies and qualifications necessary to run the business successfully. More and more family owners see the importance of learning general skills (self-management, people skills, and technical skills) and practical knowledge outside the family business. However, a concern about sending family members outside the family firm is the uncertainty of their return. I know the best thing I ever did was to work outside the business before returning. My father was also pleased that I made mistakes using other people's money rather than our own! My children and nieces and nephews will be expected to do the same: hopefully more of the outside learning than the mistakes. What they gain will benefit them and our business, whether they return in operational roles or not. They will likely be better owners.

What about hiring outside candidates? Family firms can be more attractive to prospective employees because of their family atmosphere and treatment of employees as part of the family. Still, family firms sometimes face the difficulty of attracting top executives. High-potential personnel who aspire to move up the management ladder often find themselves reluctant to join these firms because they perceive their advancement opportunities as slim, given their lack of relation to the owning family. Nonfamily executives play an essential role in the family business, as they provide outside expertise in areas where family members might have limited knowledge. I will explore this in later sections, but I am reminded of the mantra of a family business leader whom I have always respected: "Ability is thicker than blood."

Marketing is another functional area in which family firms' systems differ from those of nonfamily peers. There is an increased interest in understanding, and exploiting, the positioning of "family" by family businesses. Aspirational family firms such as Hallmark, Levi's, and S.C. Johnson are synonymous with excellent marketing of their quality brands. These family firms are referred to as "brand-builders," able to create a brand that stands out as different, distinctive, and, most important, attractive. Other family firms align their marketing to highlight their perceived distinctiveness, earned over generations. Examples include Michelin, which takes pride in its revolutionary products, Adolph Coors for the quality of its beer, Cargill and Walmart for their efficient operations, and the Bechtel Group and J. P. Morgan & Co. for their deal-making ability. Thriving family firms excel not only in the strategy they pursue but also in how they market themselves to the world. This is something I have become better at myself over the years. My stakeholders, including employees, suppliers, financiers, and customers, value that we are, and intend to stay, a family business.

Growth Strategy

While I have argued here that structures and systems are different in family firms like ours, recall my main thesis that structures and systems are in place to furnish the strategy. Strategies come in various flavors and could be, for example, differentiation strategy or consolidation strategy. The one that I would like to focus on in this chapter is growth strategy.

The topic of growth, I think, fits in well with architecture. Actually, it could fit in anywhere in this book. But if you recall that the architecture needs to be top of mind when considering strategy, it makes sense to me to focus on growth as a strategy subdimension because, if it has not already, it will come onto your radar a lot as you evolve as a leader. And, trust me on this, it is not as easy to grasp as you may think, no matter what those in nonfamily business would have you believe. In the Macduff family, we have been indoctrinated with different versions of the importance of growth: "If you aren't growing you are standing still," "If you don't grow you die," and "If you aren't growing you are going backwards." I am sure these sound vaguely familiar, at least in spirit.

Regardless of ownership type, any growth strategy requires a strong financial strategy. Family businesses have been found to have long-term rather than short-term financial goals. Usually, the founding generation was focused on the survival of the business, and profits therefore flowed back into the business rather than to the founders, in order to self-fund growth. As such, family business founders are often more averse to debt burdens than their nonfamily contemporaries are, and although family firms have been found to be innovative, they have a tendency toward risk-aversion, particularly after the business is established.

One particular aspect that distinguishes family firms is how our perceived conservatism and independence manifest vis-à-vis distinctive financial policies despite the desire for growth. If you are like me, you are not interested in sharing ownership with shareholders outside the family. I, like many I know, am open to nonfamily participation but do not wish to relinquish control. I prefer to use retained earnings or bank loans to finance growth.

Someone heard of my fascination with this topic and asked me to address the growth question mentioned earlier at a gathering of family business leaders. The picture that emerged from the family firms in attendance was that while all had experienced growth, how they measured growth varied. The basis for such variation can in some instances be traced to industry group. For example, in the case of a construction firm, the owner discussed growth in terms of assets while families engaged in manufacturing enterprises tended to measure growth in terms of employees. All, of course, did accept the many facets of growth, but their divergent immediate reactions to the question "how do you know you have grown?" were quite interesting. Apart from their diverse industry groupings, a common pattern of what growth aspects to concentrate on at various stages in the development of their family firms did emerge. Allow me to elaborate.

Simply put, growth can be conceived of as a form of organization transition that meets the needs of the business at any point in its particular development stage. In its early stages of development this is most likely measured in terms of *sales* growth and *market share* growth. To successfully service these increased market demands, then, requires additional *human resources,* and therefore growth at this stage is typically measured in terms of increases in employees. As businesses grow in these ways, the requirement for increased levels of *working capital* makes *cash flow* growth a critical success factor. Subsequently *profit* growth emerges as the means by which the business sustains itself and provides a basis for further growth and development. Accordingly, growth measures are best understood in terms of the development life cycle and are the measures that ensure survival at the particular stage and facilitate movement to the next stage of development should the family business so desire. While these are the different measures of growth, I am of the belief that family businesses have to settle upon how they are going to pursue growth, however measured.

The options for family firms include both internal and external growth strategies. Internal growth is largely achieved through the development of new products and outlets or territories. In the current era of the globalization of business, one of the best avenues to achieve *internal growth* is through the development of export markets. Developing an export market now represents one of the most attractive growth options for small- and medium-sized family firms. But this is dependent on location and industry, among other influences. Regardless, I do know that there is evidence indicating that family firms tend to rely on product (and service) differentiation strategies to gain their competitive advantage and thus grow. In other words, they tend not to seek to grow through offering the lowest price in the market but instead rely on some form of differentiation to attract a price premium. Growing internally is for many considered the safest alternative. It is not without challenges, particularly and perhaps not surprisingly as it relates to the systemic changes mentioned earlier that need to be addressed. More specifically, growing internally typically exerts strain on the firm's human resource and financial systems, and understanding this in advance has helped me appreciate the importance of planning strategically.

This is something I had to learn the hard way. Recall my grandfather died in the early stages of our company, and my father effectively rode a growth wave where opportunities abounded. He was supported by a sometimes-reluctant banking community and a dedicated and loyal staff. But he wasn't one for looking too far ahead nor renowned for his formalized planning processes. I observed early in my 10-year apprenticeship how decisions were made and committed myself to changing this process. I knew that in order to succeed we needed to continue to grow and, important, that this required a combination of internal and external growth approaches. But, more important, I knew that growth was not a reactionary process; it is proactive and deliberate, particularly in my situation, as I was accountable to some family owners who did not think that growth was necessary, no matter the form. Early on I found that I could convince them that internal growth was fundamental to our survival but have found the conversation and the actual undertaking of external growth more difficult. But there is a science to it, as I will now attempt to explain.

External growth is achieved through the acquisition of other firms. Family businesses can grow dramatically through acquisitions so long as they learn the rules of the game and avoid management hubris. After building a successful company that has a sound competitive position and strong market niche through sheer hard work, it may be difficult to grow further internally, or what is sometimes referred to as "organically." It is in this situation that family firms can consider using their financial and management resources to buy another company. But, though this is changing in the current environment where there seems to be a lot of private equity money around, while a great deal is known about the acquisition of public companies much less is known about the buying and selling of private businesses. That being the case, a key factor in overcoming the problems and seizing the opportunities in private company acquisitions is access to and utilization of essential information. I will detail this briefly here, but if you really want to know more about how all this works, investigate the process employed by what are now known as *search funds,* which have grown in prominence in recent years.

While for quite a long time many were of the opinion that family firms were hesitant to pursue diversification strategies, this seems to be no longer the case as industry disruptions are causing uncertainty in many established family businesses. Increasingly, it seems growth through acquisition is on the table as a way to address risk concerns. And, therefore, there is a need to formulate a successful acquisition strategy. It is very much on my strategic planning agenda, which has caused me to consider the following essential ingredients of our acquisition strategy.

Here are the 10 observations that should be considered:

1. *Link to strategy:* An acquisition has to be part of a broader, market-based strategy for growth.
2. *Engage professionals:* At every step of the way, questions that are highly technical arise, requiring specially qualified professional assistance. Many of these technical issues need to be recognized early in the process before commitments have been made irreversible.
3. *Trust but verify:* Carefully check the credentials and capabilities of those you choose to represent you in negotiations.
4. *Identify your target:* The best acquisition targets are seldom advertised for sale.
5. *Asset value is key:* A professional valuation is essential. An appropriate method for valuing privately held companies will generally be based on fairly short-term prospects, since buyers of such companies can rarely wait five or more years for a return. In private company acquisitions, asset value will have a greater influence on selling price than it usually does in larger public company acquisitions, which are more likely to be pure earnings

plays. This is because the private company acquisition is generally riskier, and it is correspondingly more important to have assets to sell off in the event of complete failure.

6. *Establish a fair price:* Accounting and tax conventions play a significant role in acquisition calculations. Often the money for acquisitions is borrowed, and so the pretax rate of return on assets needs to be assessed to ascertain if the purchase can be self-funding. In addition, if the acquisition strategy is well conceived and executed, there will generally be cost savings from combining operations, or increased sales by exploiting market opportunities, leading to profits high enough to fund the acquisition and a sizable sum left over to compensate for the risk of the venture.

7. *Estimate real earnings:* A related issue is making an accurate estimate of the selling company's true, as opposed to reported, earnings. The application of various accounting conventions needs to be understood in terms of the effect on the financial performance of the company.

8. *Organize the financing package:* Generally, shares in closely held companies are unacceptable to vendors; that leaves cash as the most likely acceptable form of consideration. The sources of cash will be equity or debt. Equity funds can come from current shareholders as additional subscriptions, but these are often out of the question for most families. Borrowing funds is the most common source for an investment of this type.

9. *Making it pay:* The success of an acquisition is based on what happens after the acquisition is made. Often this arises from what is known as the "new owner effect." A new owner brings new energy, a new perspective, and new human and financial resources to a situation that had perhaps grown stale.

10. *Understanding and blending culture:* No matter how attractive the deal looks on paper, the challenge will be to blend the two entities. This is perhaps where the architecture conversation comes back into the picture. More specifically, what changes need to be made to the systems and structures? And what can be done ahead of time to facilitate smooth integration?

My intention in including this focus on a particular type of strategy was to reinforce the relationship among structures and systems and strategy. Recall that structures dictate both organizational activities and the authority and autonomy of those designated to undertake the activities and that (1) these are inherently different in family firms and (2) will manifest in either functional, multidimensional, or matrix formats, (3) which will determine the managerial control systems and (4) the functional systems in place, including performance, human resources, and marketing.

Though that may sound convoluted, my message really is quite simple: the structures and systems furnish the pursued strategy.

Summary

The architectures (structure and systems) of family firms are different from those of nonfamily firms. As explained in the first section of this chapter, I've sought to identify those that are systematically different between family and nonfamily firms, and to illuminate those that have been evidenced as best practice. In short, these architectures typically entail (1) flatter structures that enable (2) faster decision making and (3) less sophisticated systems that are complemented by (4) clan-based controls. In the second section of the chapter, I introduced growth into the discourse as a means to highlight the architecture–strategy interplay.

Trilogy of Lessons for Best Practice Long-Term Stewardship

Lesson 1: The family sets the foundational bedrock of structures and systems.

Lesson 2: Building flexible (growth) capabilities is an owner's purview.

Lesson 3: Strategy matters and *what counts gets counted.*

Exemplar Story: Architecture

The 29-year-old G2 COO of her family's packaging company felt as if she had "been through a fifteen-round boxing match wrapped in a long marathon." Since her MBA graduation two and a half years earlier, she had worked intensely with her father and sister to turn around the declining fortunes of the B2B company her father, the current CEO, had bought when she was growing up. The company was owned 100 percent by her G1 father and mother.

At the time of her reentry to the business after graduating, the company had posted a second consecutive annual net loss. Its costs were out of line, and it lacked a coherent sales strategy. The company desperately needed to respond to shifts in its customers' industries, which were buffeted by global consolidation, increasingly sophisticated marketing, and cheaper manufacturing from China. She felt that the tenured management team that reported to her father was an impediment to these changes.

With 80 percent of the organization reporting to her, she knew that structures were her highest priority. She needed to know who would be able to adapt to the reorganization and who would not. To alleviate anxieties over the new changes and to deliver a consistent message, the COO, her father, and sister conducted meetings with the functional departments to explain the new organization structure, the direction of the company, and the changes that were expected. They also made sure to present a unified front throughout the transition to make sure that employees received a consistent message.

In the end, 16 percent of the supervisors were let go or resigned. The COO promoted from within those she felt had the skills and talent to lead a team but had not had the opportunity because of the entrenched management.

During the reorganization process, the COO leveraged the newly created outside board of advisors to help give her legitimacy with the rest of the organization. She announced the board's creation, introduced the advisors to the company, and made sure they were very visible during the transition. The first board meeting was on-site, and senior managers were invited to the meeting so they could ask questions and the board could get a feel of the management team. "It made a tremendous difference that three senior-looking executives were seen walking through the facilities during that period, and that I was going to be accountable to someone else besides a family member," the COO said.

The sister was promoted to vice president of sales and focused on developing relationships with the new consolidated customer giants. The new companies relied more and more on sophisticated retailing and marketing know-how and less on the personal relationships that had characterized the industry during its infancy and that had given the company some of its initial marketing advantages.

The father and sister suspected that the company's image within the industry had not evolved. In fact, "two potential global customers had a negative perception of the company," according to the sister. As vice president of sales, she reintroduced the family business to the brands across the continent and hired eight staff members to be closer to the customers. Gradually the business changed its image from a low-cost packaging provider to an innovative, integrated company offering a complete turnkey solution for new product development.

At the urging of the board of advisors, the company began to investigate manufacturing capabilities in Asia. After several trips over a span of 18 months, the COO identified a key supplier that would keep the firm cost-competitive and signed an exclusive development agreement. She explained, "The real benefit is that this gives us a viable supply-chain strategy. It also gives us the opportunity to develop more new products. It used to cost us $250,000 for tooling and molding for each new product. In Asia, it's $25,000. We can develop and test ten new products for what it used to cost us to develop one. Ninety percent of the decision is our ability to launch more new products."

Fundamental changes had been implemented. According to the COO, "The organization is aligned; we have the right people in place for day-to-day operations; we have the right customer strategy with relationships with the six to eight largest brands; our costs are under control; and we have a viable supply-chain strategy going forward."

In the process of turning around the business, the three family members were satisfied with how they communicated and made joint decisions. They were able to bounce ideas off each other for reality checks. The sisters discussed business together over lunch every day and developed a high level of trust. All three family members found feedback from the board to be very valuable, too.

Faced with the exciting prospects of growth, all three family members were surprised to discover that they were not in agreement on the direction of the company and that this was causing a real impasse. The COO thought staff needed to grow in the sales area first. Her sister, the vice president of sales, thought that staff growth was needed on the operations side first. Their father, the CEO, thought that both areas need to grow concurrently. The COO was frustrated by the impasse. "It's been frustrating that none of us is 100 percent clear what the direction needs to be. I know we have a board meeting in a few months, and we need to have a plan, but if we can't, we need to take this situation to the board."

Another issue was on the minds of the sisters: while there was a common understanding that an ownership transfer of the business to the siblings would eventually happen, the timing and mechanism remained unclear. Bringing up such a sensitive family issue seemed like a delicate matter. Yet not putting the issue on the agenda relegated the topic behind more immediate pressing problems that always needed solving.

This exemplar story is based on the following case study: John L. Ward and Canh Tran, *Generational Transition and Transformation*, unpublished case, Kellogg School of Management, 2006.

Stewart's Takeaways from the Exemplar Story: Architecture

- *To change the trajectory of the business, the family changed the architecture of the enterprise.*
- *As other areas of concern arise (moving manufacturing overseas, future transfer of leadership and ownership), the new architecture provides a platform for improved decision making.*
- *Yet new architecture cannot be static. It needs to change with future (family and business) issues and opportunities.*

CHAPTER THREE

Governance

Keeping the family engaged, educated and entrepreneurial gets harder as the family grows and disperses. Without engagement, the entrepreneurial energy of the next generation dissipates or is redirected into nonfamily business opportunities. Or, in many cases, a lack of engagement leads to the sale of the family business. The role of the family, often through its governance system, is to harness that energy and direct it inward to the family business.

—Sylvia Shepard, Fifth-Generation Owner,
Menasha Corporation

Before we dive into this conversation, let me remind you of one critical thing: all firms are governed. Then, given that, it is reasonable to suggest that the concept of governance has been around as long as there has been commerce. However, the topic of governance and the term "governance" have gained prominence comparatively only recently.

As a leader of family business I have been long fascinated by governance, in general. This is in part, I admit, because I want my nonfamily corporate counterparts to see me as professional. But my interest in the topic began well before I took on my leadership role. I've been a keen student of long-lived family firms that have been able to survive multiple generational transitions. Through careful study I've observed that the one thing the vast majority of them spend a lot of time on is governance; this piqued my interest as I was serving my apprenticeship en route to my leader's chair. In this chapter I'll share my multidimensional perspective on governance as related to the family enterprise.

Governance in Family Firms

Any introductory session on governance will likely position it as referring to the specific structures, systems, and processes that provide direction, control, and accountability for an enterprise, to promote unity and
commitment of ownership. For family enterprises, mine included, the
mixture of business, family, and ownership concerns makes governance
more challenging than in nonfamily businesses, as this overlap often
leads to a greater divergence of views on how the firm should be run, the
direction it should take, and the steps needed to achieve its goals.

For the family, governance is a means to protect the family wealth and
preserve the family legacy, for generations to come. Governance systems
are used to direct and control an organization for and on behalf of the
owners. They are built on an interlocking framework of rules, relationships, structures, systems, and processes within and by which organizational authority is exercised and controlled. Understanding the unique
governance dynamics of family business requires distinguishing between
business governance and family governance.

In Chapter 2, which covered Architecture, I discussed various organizational structures/processes primarily in the *management* sense. Here, in the
governance dimension of my AGES framework, I'll focus on the structures/
processes needed to provide oversight of the direction, control, and
accountability functions of the family and the firm. It is important to stress
again that *all* firms have established governance systems, structures, and
processes, though these are sometimes quite informal.

Understanding the role of governance has been important to me for
two main reasons:

1. First, our firm's governance provides stakeholders, including me, with a
   sense of direction for the business, with focus on the vision. Fundamental,
   then, is an appreciation that those who are charged with governance responsibilities become the developers and guardians of the firm's vision.

2. Second, governance is the process of setting the values by which those
   involved with the (family) business live and work. This is especially important in the context of a multigenerational family business. As the family and
   business evolve and face transition between generations, guiding policies
   help to influence behavior because, typically, individuals interpret visions
   and values in their own idiosyncratic way. Thus, it's vital to ensure that each
   member of the organization understands and accepts the policies in place to
   direct the family and the business.

Based on the aforementioned ideas, governance has been vital for me
in the management of the relationships among the stakeholders who play

key roles in our firm's performance and, ultimately (hopefully), our survival and continuity. While the executive management has a reasonable level of authority to run our business, governance ensures that such authority is bounded in order to minimize executives' misuse of authority to serve their personal objectives, which are assumed but not necessarily in the best interest of owners and other stakeholders. Therefore, it's no surprise, perhaps, that the majority of what I've read on governance gravitates toward the function of monitoring the performance of the management. While this aspect is, and continues to be, important, reducing the proportion of time devoted to monitoring may enable the board to devote more time and effort to other areas that add more value to the firm.

Important in this context, given the overlap of management, family, and ownership (those three circles again!), management's self-interested behavior may be less pronounced in family firms than in their nonfamily peers. One author referred to this as "clan control," which certainly resonates with me. With the assumption that family members in the business will be more steward-like in their orientation, given that their expectations are clarified and there is strong trust in the relationship, there is no need for as great an investment in monitoring, and the board can work with the CEO and management team to create value and wealth for, and on behalf of, the owners. The firm leadership and decision-makers can then move forward and focus more on *lead* indicators rather than be obsessed about *lag* indicators, which they can no longer influence. Such focus is conducive to moving from a short-term to a longer-term orientation.

Relatedly, trust is crucial in the organization. To establish this precious commodity, the most important aspect is the need for *clarity,* or making sure that management and, where one exists, the board of directors understand their roles and responsibilities. In fact, I and others like to say that the aim of governance is "to build trust in a team of decision-making teams." The board and senior management need to identify what problems are located in the board's arena as opposed to the management's. It is even more challenging for family members who have concurrent executive and governance roles. Oftentimes, they shift nearly seamlessly from one to the other—such as going from the production floor to sit in a board meeting while they're still thinking about operations! That can be an issue because the board's responsibility is to envisage the future and think about where to take the organization, rather than to focus on operational issues, unless in situations where operational issues place the business at significant risk. Having directors overinvolved in operations makes no sense, as executives are paid good money to manage this function.

Put simply, my board of directors has two important roles to fulfill:

1. Performance
2. Conformance

The board has the responsibility to oversee the firm's performance for shareholders through strategy formulation and policymaking. Directors are also tasked to ensure compliance, or conformance, with the firm's relevant legal framework by monitoring the company and self-regulating their own conduct individually and collectively as a board. One leader I know whose family struggled for some time with his board's role told me he ultimately concluded, "It is just another form of insurance . . . and it is the cheapest premium I pay."

I remind the board, via the cover page of every board meeting agenda, that our *raison d'etre* can be captured under four major functions, and remembering this will help us avoid getting "into the weeds" during our increasingly precious time together. The four areas are as follows:

1. *Value creation:* The board's role is to ensure that the enterprise creates long-term, sustainable value. This can be accomplished by making available to management the resources needed to achieve the agreed-on strategic plan (into which the board previously had development input).
2. *Appointment of the CEO:* Recruiting, overseeing, and evaluating the CEO is one of the board's most crucial functions. The board also appoints the senior management to carry out day-to-day activities within the framework of established policies and strategic guidelines.
3. *Performance improvement:* Through strategy formulation and policymaking, the board guides management and ensures that performance improves continuously.
4. *Monitoring performance:* Together with performance improvement, the board periodically reviews established policies, goals, strategies, and performance targets with management to ensure that the firm is aligned with its vision. Risks should also be identified and managed by the board.

Fundamentally, and this also helps focus our attention in the boardroom, there are three core strategy-linked questions that should be asked continually at the board level:

1. Where are we now?
2. Where do we want to go?
3. How do we get there?

The board needs to ask these deceptively simple questions repeatedly to know and analyze the firm's real circumstance at any point. This reinforces my claim in the previous chapter about the importance of *planning*.

Before I proceed in this section, I need to stress that families who are serious about governance understand that one of the key features that distinguishes them is the capability to be flexible in how they approach the design of their governance structures. But, given the aforementioned functions, the next governance consideration I've had is related to board *structure* and *composition*. Ultimately, the specific characteristics of an individual firm determine its board's structure. However, multiple factors determine the number of directors required, including the number set in the company's constitution and the firm's size, along with the organizational type and structure. As mentioned earlier, the structures and processes in the business could range from informal to formal, depending on its current development stage. White Board Illustration 3.1 shows the firm's business-governance structural options. In the course of its life through multiple generations, a typical family business will move through these board forms in a sequence of stages.

As a family enterprise leader I was well aware of the assertion that appointing independent (nonfamily) directors to family business boards improves board functioning and adds value to the business. While I had a gut feel this principle was valid, I had difficulty locating systematic evidence that independent directors do in fact add discernible value to family business board processes. My comfort zone, therefore, became simply to look beyond the "independence" of a director and rather at the key capabilities each brings to the table. In particular, I was advised that

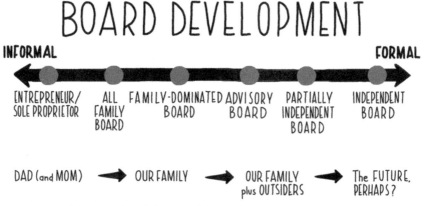

White Board Illustration 3.1. Board Development

independence of thought and their understanding of—and willingness to provide—*accountability* are essential qualities to seek in all directors. Therefore, stressing these capabilities rather than focusing solely on their origins should lead to improved board performance and has in my experience.

In terms of composition and size, thriving family businesses, and I now count mine in this mix, are seen to have *smaller* boards rather than large ones. As independence of thought and accountability are key principles in governance, as noted earlier, it is beneficial if the majority of directors are independent outsiders and not friends of the family or coming from any of the firm's service providers. It is in the independence of thought and accountability that the board can create value for the firm by avoiding the influence of a small number of family members who may not have the enterprise's overall best interests in mind.

As a final consideration regarding board membership, I have found that family business governance is the most contentious issue in family firms because different members of the family are often desirous of becoming members of the board. Often, even when their preparation, skills, capabilities, and competencies are not necessarily well developed, they may still feel they deserve a board seat because they are representing their branch of the family. Whatever members' reasons for wanting to be part of governance, all family members need the insight and understanding to appreciate that their responsibility is to the *business,* not to the constituency that put them on the board. I cannot stress this enough and will never tire of reminding family members of it, along with anyone else who will listen.

Notwithstanding the aforementioned ideas, I am convinced that fixating on matters such as independent boards tends to overshadow the issue truly at the heart of corporate governance challenges worldwide: accountability. Accountability is the need for decision-makers to justify and accept responsibility for their decisions and how these are implemented (or not). For family firms, accountability also entails avoiding conflicts between family members' roles in the family and their roles in business, while preserving an overall atmosphere of trust and unity.

While the principles for governance are equally applicable in the contexts of family and nonfamily business, *how* accountability is rendered in a family business differs from its treatment in a public company. Specifically, the so-called models of accountability in a public arena do not necessarily transfer to private firms. The observed differences between widely held companies and family firms include that while the former tend to be fragmented and management-driven, with impersonal ownership and boards focused on protecting the interests of owners, the family firm community is characterized by concentrated, personal ownership, ownership-driven direction, and boards servicing the interests of owners and managers.

Regardless, to achieve accountability, the board must possess the wherewithal necessary to ensure it is accountable to shareholders. There must also be established ways for shareholders to exert their rights in order to hold the board accountable. Most important, the board must also be aware of means of holding management accountable for its actions.

For publicly listed companies, the riding instructions for the board are relatively straightforward: to generate positive returns consistent with the firm's risk profile. Apart from the ease of knowing these homogeneous expectations, the board also has the comfort of knowing that there is a ready avenue for any disaffected owners to sell their shares and move their capital to a company more in keeping with their expectations. In the case of family businesses, these conditions of known homogeneous expectations and ready liquidity for ownership transfers often do not prevail. Therefore, the role of director of a family business can be more challenging. Given that many owners are "locked in" as shareholders with limited or restricted exit options, there is a necessity to make sure that the board is acting on behalf of all shareholders. Thus, the board needs to understand what the shareholders' expectations are.

Moreover, in firms with family ownership, shareholders' connection to the firm is more than economic. Public company shareholders and perhaps smaller nonfamily private firm shareholders can be assumed to have homogeneous expectations that are financially based. But when the connection to the firm is both emotional and economic, as is the case for family business shareholders, the identification of their more heterogeneous expectations becomes a necessary prerequisite for good governance.

Corporate governance principles typically specify that the board should promote the interests of the company, the interests of the shareholders, or the interests of both. Control model countries typically promote company interests, while market model countries typically promote the shareholders' immediate interest. However, for family-controlled businesses, over and above these particular issues of direction, control, and accountability, the way in which the board governs the family business, hopefully, promotes family trust and unity as well. Keeping the business on track and trying to accommodate diverse expectations of family members is a challenge for the board. It shouldn't be that, in going forward, the family is not as committed to the enterprise because of its quality of governance or that they become disillusioned with what the business is doing. Thus, it becomes an obligation for those entrusted with the company's governance not only to direct and control it but also to harmonize the family and maintain the family as committed owners of the firm.

The Importance of Independence

Introducing governance initiatives is not without its challenges. For example, the leader of a substantial family business told me his father's reply when he told his father they should modify governance structures and processes, including adding independent directors: "Certainly, Son. I welcome your proposal. Please, when you submit it, be sure to attach your letter of resignation." It will surely take time to get the incumbents' buy-in. But as another wise soul reminisced, "I should have done it [bring in independent directors] much sooner." Still another said, "It is a no brainer . . . takes the pressure off me to have people who the family trusts to help me guide the business . . . and besides everything else you may hear . . . if you want to sleep well at night and get along with your family members, put independent directors on your board."

Fortunately, recent evidence about boards and performance tends to substantiate my approach based on the principles *of independence of thought* and *accountability*. Specifically, there's still no direct link between systematic governance structure and financial performance, but growing data on how the effects of board structure and composition on firm performance are more indirect and complex. Therefore, the processes by which directors *interact* with one another have become the focus. Specifically, we now know how structure, group processes, and outside directors in family firms positively affect board processes: a greater proportion of outside board members is associated with higher levels of *effort norms* and *board cohesion*—board-level processes that are likely to enhance board effectiveness; that is, boards with outside directors are perceived as more committed to the board's tasks (i.e., higher effort norms) and are more cohesive. Also, the boards of larger and older family companies demonstrated more clearly than those of other family firms the positive effects of outside directors on *effort, cohesion,* and *use of knowledge and skills.*

Therefore, when I have been required to appoint independent directors to the board of our family business, I examine closely their ability to promote accountability and their ability to generate new ideas and challenge the board's strategic plan. With these selection criteria, my family board has indeed shown higher levels of effort norms and board cohesion, which in turn have resulted in a more effective board. In time this should positively influence our broader enterprise performance.

I have often been asked about the cost of this "additional" governance; I can firmly attest that it is the cheapest advice you can buy. Don't focus on the cost; focus on the benefit(s). Even a single insightful direction from an independent director will repay his or her fees many times over. Having independents on the board changes how I approach my leadership role. I am more accountable for my actions (and behavior), and that message has cascaded through our business and the family.

The other question I get often is, "How many independents is the right number?" The answer to this is, "Ultimately, no fewer than three"—but you need to crawl before you walk before you run. It will probably take time to get your show sufficiently in order to attract high-caliber independents, and I recommend you start the journey with an advisory board. You and everyone involved, particularly incumbents who are stuck in their ways, need to get comfortable with the idea of sharing information with outsiders, and an advisory board will smooth the way to a more formal, fiduciary board. I was reminded early on to "be careful you not hit a nut with a sledgehammer," which effectively means that the approach should be aligned with the need.

Why three independents? Basically, this will ensure you have a quorum for them to discuss issues and, from a logistics point of view, there will almost always be two independents present for board meetings (schedule conflicts could prevent one independent from joining quarterly meetings). Having at least three is also helpful when, inevitably, board members retire. If you plan it correctly, succession in the boardroom is not an issue and you will smoothly transition individuals off the board, which is vital for regeneration of ideas as the needs of the business evolve.

"How many family members should be on the board?" is another common query. As someone I respect told me bluntly, "It doesn't matter, as long as there are three *independents*." But he also followed up to explain that a board should be no more than eight members, and to remember that the director's responsibility by law is to the business, not to the constituency that put him or her there.

Believe me, when you see good directors in action, you'll know what I mean. They leave any biases at the door and come prepared to every meeting to "persuade and be persuaded." They are caring, constructive critics who are keen thinkers understanding the family's values and the business's culture. They don't overstay their welcome. One leader of a family business I know serves on other family boards under one condition, about which he is adamant: "You get me for five years, no more . . . use and abuse me for that time . . . as after five years my experience is that no one is truly independent and I don't want to be that guy who hangs around too long. As we approach the five-year mark I know I will be too enmeshed with the family and they need someone who is clearly objective. If needed I make myself available for *ad hoc* direction and mentorship . . . but not in the formal capacity as an independent nonfamily non-executive director."

Owners' Responsibilities

For nonfamily firms as well as family businesses, there is often a different level of emphasis among and mix of types of owners. Some are *operating owners,* taking part in the management and operations of the business. Others are *governing owners,* focusing mostly on the direction and control of the business. There are also those who are *investing owners,* who hold shares in the firm while allowing the management and board to carry out what needs to be done.

For family firms, however, the overlap of ownership and control creates two critical challenges for the owners:

1. How to be watchful and contribute to the family business.
2. How to forge a consensus and common voice of family ownership opinion.

The real need for active family business owners is to create harmony among ownership, family, and management systems, and to foster and enhance positive family–business relations. Popular consensus is that family business owners have four broad responsibilities:

1. To define the *values* that shape the company's culture by having regular sessions with the managers
2. To set the *vision* that establishes the parameters and boundaries for management strategies
3. To specify the *financial targets* around growth, risk, liquidity, and profitability that the board can evaluate for feasibility and consistency
4. To elect the *directors* and design the board

The unification of ownership and control has driven me to establish family governance structures and processes, in order to add value to the business, particularly in fostering positive business–family interaction. But, as I capture in White Board Illustration 3.2, this is a dynamic process.

GOVERNANCE PROCESS FRAMEWORK

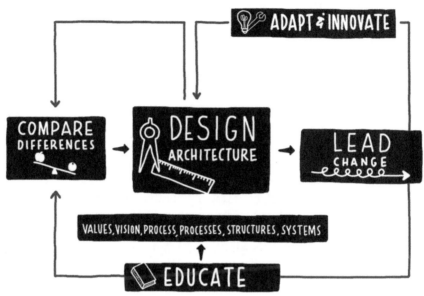

White Board Illustration 3.2. Governance Process Framework

Family Governance Structure and Process

What family governance structures and processes should be in place for family firms, given the earlier discussion? For some family firms, especially those still in the founder stage, the usual practice is for family leaders to make family governance decision themselves, without consulting other members. Some founders poll the family, asking them what they think, and make an informed decision thereafter. Particularly as the family grows, there is generally a need for structures, either formal or informal, to deliver family governance in the firm, providing *education* and fostering *communication* within the family business. This can be achieved through holding family meetings, convening a family assembly, or establishing a family council, with the support of a family charter or constitution.

The *Family Council* is the governance body focusing on family affairs. It serves the family, just as the board of directors serves the business. The role of the Family Council is to promote communication among family members and to provide a forum for the resolution of family conflicts. Moreover, the council supports the education of next-generation members. We have a Family Council, which is chaired by my aunt and populated by members of the third generation.

A *Family Assembly* is useful when the size of the family prevents all from sitting on the Family Council. An annual assembly operates in conjunction with the Family Council. Even if convened only once a year, the Family Assembly is another vehicle for education, communication, and renewal of family bonds. Through the assembly, family members are given opportunities to participate and learn about the family business. With a growing number of family, we are getting to the stage that we need to introduce a Family Assembly. It is on the agenda for the Family Council.

To govern the relationships between the owners, family members, and managers, in our family, we have developed a *Family Charter* (sometimes called a *Family Constitution*). The document explicates some of the principles and guidelines owners (shareholders) follow in their relations with each other, other family members, and managers. Our Family Charter has no legal bearing but refers to documents that do (company constitution, buy–sell agreements, etc.). Important, in drafting our Family Charter, we were reminded that no amount of legal expertise can match the goodwill and personal responsibility of family members. It was hard work, but the process was rewarding on many levels.

The F-Suite and C-Suite

As you may have concluded by now, the topic of governance has become a passion of mine. Most recently, my white board musing has captured the differences in terms of the *F-Suite* and *C-Suite*. I maintain that those involved in family governance need both a "Family-Suite" skillset (to navigate complex relationships and communicate amid diverse expectations and so on) and a C-Suite mind-set (to be equipped with enough commercial

White Board Illustration 3.3. F-Suite and C-Suite

smarts to appreciate the demands of a growing business). Conversely, those in the C-Suite (including those involved in governing the business) need to have a C-Suite skillset and an F-Suite mind-set (to understand the nuances of family enterprise, including long-term orientation, family values, and importance of having many stakeholders). White Board Illustration 3.3 represents this with a Yin-Yang symbol.

Summary

I have provided an overview of the business and family governance structures and processes for family as compared to nonfamily businesses. The governance of family business is arguably more difficult than that in firms with more widely dispersed owners. Specifically, I've found that my family as owners increasingly have different expectations of the business and, at the same time, also have limited opportunities to either influence others or liquidate their ownership relative to public company shareholders. Therefore, I embarked on a dual journey not only to introduce business governance to us but also to complement it carefully with family governance. The family governance, through education and communication, clarified the economic and emotional expectations family owners had of the business. Family governance thus became our "market" for expectations. These distilled expectations then became the riding instructions for the business governance directors. They accepted the challenge to be accountable to family owners for performing according to these expectations and held management accountable by challenging them with strong independence of thought. We now enjoy much better integrated family business governance.

Trilogy of Lessons for Best Practice Long-Term Stewardship

Lesson 1: Governing the family is arguably more difficult (and more important) than governing the business.

Lesson 2: Independence of thought is crucial, and this includes having outsiders as members of the board to garner unbiased objective views.

Lesson 3: Owners' expectations need to be interpreted with commercial realism.

Exemplar Story: Governance

A large banking and ranching family enterprise in the mountain states of the United States was shifting leadership from the five-sibling plus spouse generation (G2) to 19-cousin plus spouse's generation (G3). There were already 30 members of G4.

Elders had worked hard to engage family members with the business and with each other. Each year, they convened to celebrate their unity, share their joy with each other, and appreciate their diversity. They were proactive—had launched a cousins' camp, published a newsletter, and collected and archived their heritage. They had adopted a family constitution, defined their values, and clarified their family's vision and mission. They created a Family Council (FC) to serve the mission, a council of elders to mentor younger members, a family office to support financial planning and personal development, and a human resource system to develop succession and leadership plans.

A decision was made that within a year, the roles of CEO at both the bank and the ranch would for the first time be nonfamily executives, already tapped. No longer would G2 members be active in the management of the family enterprises and a new mixture of nonfamily top management and second- and third-generation family board members would guide the businesses. The third generation of cousins was eager to take a more active role in the governance of the various family enterprises.

The family had developed a protocol that was agreed upon by all to select family board members for their various entities (bank, ranch, foundation, family council) by "one family" as opposed to branches. Yet when the selection of two family representatives to the banking board occurred, three were actually elected, which was not in accordance with the protocol. A G3 family member questioned why the selection rules were changed by G2 members without input or vote?

> It pains me to see how the latest election process and the actions of the second generation will surely fragment our family further. The entire family endured a painful process to develop guidelines for elections and qualifications for these posts. The Family Council and second generation do not have the right to rewrite these rules without the consent of the Family Assembly. . . . A policy was developed that was voted on and accepted by the Family Council on how the election process would be conducted, and that too was also not adhered to by the Family Council. . . . Only two posts were available for the bank board, so why were there three candidates selected? What has recently transpired has the real potential to move us apart.

What occurred was that during the meeting in which all the G2s were to vote, it became evident for the first time that in selecting two family representatives to the board meant that one or more G2 family members would have to vote against their own G3 offspring. That realization caused the breakdown of the process.

Two months later, the FC met to review its board nomination and selection process, and also to develop a new integrated governance framework for its enterprises. The FC chairman, who was the youngest of the G2s, knew the family *was eager to explore ways to improve the process to choose family members for director positions following the emotional experience of the bank board nominations. All agreed that family decisions would be easier to accept if it was perceived that the process to make those decisions was fair. With upcoming board elections for the ranch, the bank foundation, and the FC, the family resolved to repair earlier damage and to move forward as a unified, enterprising family.*

Bank management was actively engaged in a strategic planning process, exploring ways to grow the bank both internally and externally, with new acquisitions a priority. The team at the ranch was considering major restructuring that would reduce the scope of the business, cut costs, and substantially trim the ranch's debt. Now more than ever the enterprises needed to know the expectations of family shareholders. A G3 member and vice chairman of the FC said:

> *We as a family need to understand the risks in our companies. Whatever strategy the bank pursues, we should make sure that we can understand and support it. We need to ask what it means for a business to be owned by our Family, what is unique about that, and what key strategic issues the company is facing.*

Another G3 cousin and family board director at the bank added, "We worked hard to keep the businesses family-owned. And if the five families want to keep and maintain our enterprises then it should be done intentionally."

The FC chairman pondered the best way to coordinate family expectations and to communicate them with the bank and the ranch. "We are continually striving to understand as a family how to manage our companies and to be good stewards of our assets," he said.

Here are the guidelines that the family created:

- *No surprises—everyone knows the issue and the call to decision beforehand.*
- *No conflicts of interest—personal interest and agendas are disclosed.*
- *No rush—everyone feels that they have time to prepare and time to present their views.*
- *Sincere care—each participant feels respected and heard.*
- *Mutual commitment—genuine effort to find "win–win" solutions before vote or decision.*
- *Good conduct—proceed as if meetings are videotaped to shown to future generations.*
- *Objective outsiders—independent directors/family facilitators represent interests of all.*
- *Post-decision review—everyone discusses the process and agrees to review results later.*

This exemplar story is based on the following case study: John Ward and Canh Tran, *Scott Family Enterprises (A): Defining Fair Process for Cousin Owners*, Kellogg Case #5-204-267(A), published 2004.

Stewart's Takeaways from the Exemplar Story: Governance

- *There is no "one way" to approach governance in the family and the business.*
- *Governance process is fluid, not fixed, depending on stage, complexity, and intent of the enterprise. Regardless, integrating family and business governance is complex.*
- *Family member commitment and capabilities will vary.*
- *Having written guidelines is important.*

CHAPTER FOUR

Entrepreneurship

Everything now being done is going to be done differently and it's going to be done better, and if we don't do it, our competitors will.
—Frederik Meijer, Second-Generation Leader, Meijer, Inc.

Though I consider myself to be entrepreneurial, I've always found entrepreneurship to be a loaded concept. Perhaps I inherited this attitude from my grandfather. As the founder of our family business, he undoubtedly was an entrepreneur. But, like many of his generation, he would have been reluctant to be labeled as such. Same goes for my father—the topic of entrepreneurship is just one of the many things about which he has a strong opinion (most are fodder for other books!). Part of the issue is that in their eras, entrepreneurs were not adulated, as they are these days. In fact, even in today's environment, which celebrates entrepreneurship, many still do not equate entrepreneurship with family enterprise. I used to wonder why this is so, but over time I've developed clearer thinking on the matter: *family firms are entrepreneurial—we just do entrepreneurship differently.*

The best way I have found to approach a big topic like entrepreneurship is to break it down into bite-sized pieces. Or, as the professors drilled into me, "Stewart, in order to conquer a big topic, you need to divide it into understandable dimensions." Accordingly, I've divided entrepreneurship into two dimensions: entrepreneurial *strategy* and entrepreneurial *leadership*. The focus of this chapter will be on entrepreneurial strategy, as I will dive more deeply into the concept of the entrepreneurial leader in a later chapter.

Entrepreneurial Orientation and Long-Term Orientation

To understand and explain entrepreneurship in family versus nonfamily businesses, I have obsessed myself with the concept of entrepreneurial orientation (EO) and in particular how this applies to the family business context. The original measurement of the EO construct, which is based on the processes, practices, and decision-making approaches of firms that act entrepreneurially, suggested three main dimensions:

1. Innovativeness
2. Proactivity
3. Risk-taking

Innovativeness is a firm's tendency to engage in and support new ideas, novelty, experimentation, and creative processes that result in new products, services, or technological processes. *Proactivity* refers to the propensity to compete aggressively and proactively with industry rivals. *Risk-taking* is about the tendency of a firm's top management to take risks related to investment decisions and strategic choices in the face of uncertainty.

The studies I've read suggest each of these three dimensions varies independently of the others. This says to me that an entrepreneurial firm's levels of the three dimensions will differ and their relative positions will likely change over time. I relate to this, as I know my firm differs significantly from what it looked like 10 years ago on all three EO dimensions, and it definitely has diverged from the business my (very opinionated) dad stewarded.

Given this "change over time" epiphany, more recently I've been preoccupied with understanding family firms' longer-term strategic horizon. A useful way of looking at this, I believe, is by framing the conversation in another "orientation"—specifically, *long-term orientation* (LTO). This is a means to capture competitive performance advantages potentially enjoyed by families in business. And this longer-term perspective I've found, increasingly, has implications for the undertaking of entrepreneurial activities in the family firm context, mine included.

Before I address LTO, indulge me as I share something else that has preoccupied me: the related (to entrepreneurship) topic of innovation and, in particular, how family businesses face not a dilemma but a *trilemma* as they address the challenges of innovation. As an aside, while considering how to approach the topic of entrepreneurship it occurred to me that while my father did not show much interest in being labeled an entrepreneur, or even discussing the topic of entrepreneurship, he delighted in being known as an innovator. This is noteworthy, as I do think it speaks to the differences between family and nonfamily leaders, no matter their generation or industry.

Family Firms' Innovation Trilemma

Let me explain what I mean by this trilemma. There is a popular conception that family firms, by their nature, are more conservative and traditional than nonfamily firms and, as such, are not particularly accomplished innovators in terms of new products, internal processes, or marketing strategies. Respect for the family tradition, for example, tends to make managers more risk-averse and less market driven than their nonfamily-firm counterparts. Yet several contemporaries and I have taken a long-standing contrarian view on this topic, primarily because we believe there are other characteristics commonly associated with family firms that bestow the competitive advantages and operational strengths needed to be successful innovators.

Undoubtedly, innovation has always been an important component of effective, sustained family firm performance. Without a formidable (or robust) and enduring commitment to innovation, families such as Bacardi, S.C. Johnson, Michelin, Cadbury, Heineken, Coors, Mars, and Zegna would not have survived and become the brand and industry leaders we know them to be.

In their book *Managing for the Long Run,* Danny Miller and Isabelle Le Breton-Miller feature many examples of long-lived family-owned innovators and how they pursued unorthodox strategies. In their study, household names such as Michelin, W. L. Gore, Tetra Pak, and Fidelity were especially strong on what the Millers labeled a *command* dimension, or the presence of leaders who are free to make quick decisions and to seize new opportunities through innovation. For example, the firms highlighted facilitated collaboration among people from different technical and functional areas, enabling them to work together "without boundaries" to speedily create and commercialize innovations.

My fellow leaders and I have developed the notion that the interaction of family, managers, and owners creates a "trilemma" of challenges in terms of the pursuit of innovation. A trilemma suggests difficult-to-resolve tensions stemming from three arenas, leading to difficulty in choosing among three options, each of which is (or appears) unacceptable or unfavorable as a sole choice. For family innovators, these revolve around

1. leveraging *financial resources* appropriately,
2. administering *best practices* effectively, and
3. engaging *qualified personnel* impartially.

As shown in White Board Illustration 4.1, this framework can be used to create a model to account for family firm innovation strategies. The model includes three primary innovation types: new products or services, new processes, and new marketing strategies. While there are, of course, other types of innovation, I find these three most directly pertinent to innovation in our family business context.

The innovation space of family firms, like all organizations, is surrounded by external influences. These components of the external environment include (as depicted in White Board Illustration 4.1) *industry dynamics*, which include industry growth or consolidation and competition; *technological discontinuities*, which can often lead to substitute products and services; profound *changes in consumer/customer demographics*,

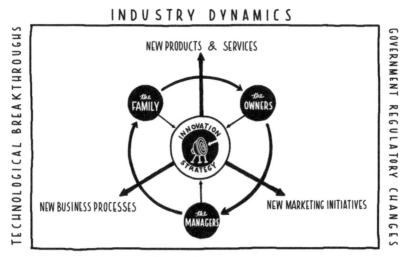

White Board Illustration 4.1. The Innovator's Trilemma Model

such as an aging population; and changes to the *regulatory regime* such as environment-related controls. Because innovation processes reflect the leading edge of changes in business and society, these external forces are especially salient to family innovators.

The genesis of this framework/model lies in the notion that the beliefs, internal dynamics, and culture of the family are pivotal to innovation outcomes. By culture, I am referring to the attitudes, belief systems, and values of the firm. With culture being readily expressed in words such as "integrity" or "privacy" or phrases such as "employees are part of the family," it is well understood that value-laden cultures can run deeply and pervasively throughout any firm. Still, it is my experience that such culture—for better or worse—runs even more deeply within family firms and is more pervasive in their day-to-day decisions because of family-owner-manager linkages.

I look at this model as a meta-system where all components are important and collectively determine the family firm's innovation strategy and outcomes. Further, and I need to keep stressing this, the components are not static but change over time. For example, the family component continues to evolve through the introduction and inevitable maturation of next-generation members and exit of the incumbents. Ownership models can also change, through both the introduction of outside investors and ownership dispersion and bequests. Further, the management of the business can change dramatically as family firms introduce nonfamily members for professional competence.

It's my experience that changes among those involved at the intersections of these three systems can readily alter a firm's innovation strategy. For example, a newer family member who has come of age and has less commitment to business continuation than his or her predecessors might well bring in a private equity firm with the intent of shaping up and positioning the firm for sale. Or, a family-dominated board, based on exposure to best practices in its industry, might opt to court a proven manager to transform a family firm in crisis. A relatively recent example of this that I followed closely was Ford Motor Company's decision (the Ford family remains the largest shareholder) to recruit Alan Mulally to lead the business. At the time, Mulally was already a world-class executive, having led the turnaround of Boeing with product innovations such as the 777 and the Dreamliner, as well as initiatives in global supply chain management. Many believe he turned around Ford, insisting on fresh designs, best-in-class quality, and new branding campaigns. The proof is in the pudding, as my wise grandfather often said: the "blue oval" company and brand have been quite successful, post-turnaround.

Importantly, even though a "traditional" family firm may seem to be operating and in many ways defining a world of its own, no family firm operates in isolation from its respective industry. External forces can impose a challenging mandate on all three trilemma components: innovate decisively or succumb. Take, for example, a fifth-generation family leader I know facing major challenges in his family's manufacturing business based on all four external environment influences in the model. Specifically, international competitors in lower-cost regimes are pioneering technologically advanced processes that enable them to introduce alternative product lines; these offerings are attractive to an increasingly discerning customer base with unprecedented buying-platform options and information-access alternatives. While his father prepared him well for his role to lead the family and the business, and though it doesn't make the challenges less palpable, one piece of advice, which defines his family's resilience in the face of adversity, has always stood out: "Even if there is no money, son, you still have to innovate and bring new products to market."

Use Polarity Mapping for Family Business Paradoxes

The aforementioned material provides me an opportunity to share a great way to conceptualize the family-business innovation/entrepreneurship dilemma of tradition-versus-change and other such paradoxes: a tool known as "polarity mapping." To put this into practice, use your white board to draw two columns and label them with the two polar extremes of the paradox in question (e.g., "tradition" and "change"). Starting with the item on the left side (tradition), list everything that represents its upside (e.g., reputation, industry knowledge), and then move to its downside (e.g., slow to react, technology laggards). Then repeat the same exercise for change, for both upside (e.g., attract fresh talent, explore new markets) and downside (e.g., risk, uncertainty among employees, confusion in marketplace).

I've captured a rough version of this polarity map in White Board Illustration 4.2. When you stand back and take a look at such a map, you'll usually see that it does not promote an "either/or" conversation. More specifically, to manage this tradition-versus-change paradox, you must establish and clearly understand that it is not "tradition or change" but "tradition *and* change"—or as one family distilled, "Change is our tradition." Another family captured this with the phrase "new ideas, old

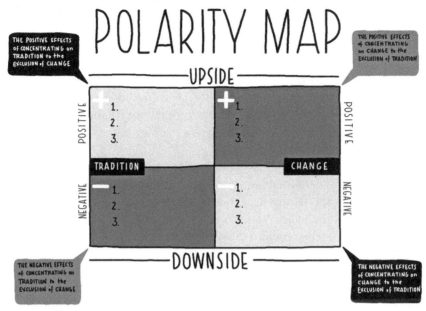

White Board Illustration 4.2. Polarity Mapping Exercise

ideals," a profound, efficient way to manage the change-tradition paradox. Polarity mapping is also very valuable for understanding others' perspective. This is a great tool for any leader and fundamental to my idea, stated earlier, of attending *Paradox School* daily.

Understand and Address the Innovation Trilemma

Despite the fact that owners, managers, and the family can bring a wealth of resources, capabilities, and insights to the innovation process, the reality is that many family firms conform to the stereotype of being innovation laggards. Within the model in White Board Illustration 4.1, family, ownership, and management can easily become tightly coupled, reinforcing unhealthy approaches to the business with respect to product, service, business process, and marketing innovation. In short, while one generation of a family firm may establish an excellent business operation, its failure to change and adapt can dampen growth. In this scenario, the family firm remains small, increasingly inconsequential over time, and subject to neglect and eventual abandonment by younger generations; once the older generation passes, the next generation is more likely to sell the assets. Indeed, this is the stereotype that many hold for a family firm's long-term prospects.

What, then, are the sources of family firm advantage, and differences, in the area of innovation? When family firms begin to stagnate, what are the special root causes that are different from or compound causes of malaise in corporations more generally? And how does the family firm sustain its innovation capability across generations? I suggest that for a family firm to become a skillful innovator, it must address a trilemma of challenges effectively.

Specifically, in White Board Illustration 4.1, the connecting arches among family-owners-managers represent important tensions that must be managed for the family firm to achieve sustained success. These tensions contribute to the family innovator's trilemma; recall from our earlier discussion that a trilemma is a difficult choice among three options, each of which is (or appears) unacceptable or unfavorable as the sole choice. My underlying thesis is that, due to the tensions arising among the three family business entities, family innovators face a level of complexity not experienced in situations without family involvement. While these conditions may introduce complexity, they also promote unique resources and operational advantages that distinguish family from nonfamily firms. And, while this complexity is challenging, in my experience, those who understand and can manage the three dilemmas associated with the three tensions are positioned to place their family's businesses in strong competitive positions over the long run.

But, after spending more time than I should have thinking about this topic, I find that the trilemma model is best understood when embedded in the aforementioned LTO frame, or that of LTO. LTO refers to the propensity of a firm to engage in long-term actions that materialize over an extended time period. Researchers have only recently begun to focus on identifying and fine-tuning the idiosyncratic family-influenced attributes associated with LTO. Among these attributes are the tendency of family firms to have CEOs with longer tenures, preference for longer investment horizons, intention to pass the business to successive generations, investment of patient capital, and transgenerational goals.

Therefore, like many who live their lives in business families, I have become an unashamed LTO zealot. LTO is formally defined as "the tendency to prioritize the long-range implications and impact of decisions and actions that come to fruition after an extended time period." Leaders charged with considering activities that orient their firms to the long term are faced with pursuing entrepreneurial activities framed in the need to consider the *future* and *continuity* of their family and business; to achieve this typically requires *perseverance* in the face of obstacles not faced by nonfamily business leaders.

Summary

While having a longer-term orientation is deemed important and helps distinguish families in businesses and the strategies they pursue, family firm leaders need to concurrently foster their competitiveness and embrace entrepreneurship. Therefore, entrepreneurship, in my AGES frame, is best defined at the intersection of entrepreneurial leadership and entrepreneurial strategy, where entrepreneurial leadership (which we will discuss in detail later) is "leadership that creates visionary scenarios that are used to assemble and mobilize a 'supporting cast' of participants who become committed by the vision to the discovery and exploitation of strategic value creation" (Lumpkin and Brigham 2011). Entrepreneurs with strong leadership abilities and insights become valuable assets, who aid the family business in achieving competitive advantage. However, important, leadership per se is insufficient unless the firm has effective strategies in place to achieve its goals. Entrepreneurial strategy is the means through which an organization establishes and reestablishes its fundamental set of relationships with its environment.

Referring to the three-systems approach introduced in the opening chapter and earlier in this chapter in the trilemma discussion, family business leaders need to consider ownership, business, and family dimensions carefully. The addition of the family system, and the associated LTO aspect, alludes to owners of family firms approaching risk differently than nonfamily business owners. My role-model leaders of multigenerational family businesses cherish enduring, open-ended, mutually beneficial relationships with business partners, customers, and broader society. They strive to ensure corporate health and continuity, exercising careful stewardship over resources and encouraging long-term executive apprenticeship and tenure. Importantly, family business leaders develop insights for the benefit of family, business, and self.

But here's the "catch" I must stress yet again. If the life cycles of the firm and the family are considered, EO has a tendency to *decrease* gradually across generations in family firms. Consider, for example, the EO dimension of risk-taking propensity. The first generation would likely have taken greater risks than the second and subsequent generations, as the latter cohorts are charged with the additional burden of stewarding the founding generation's legacy. This is not to imply that risk-taking increases but rather that new generations find new ways to perform existing operations, consistent with the notion that as successors enter the business, novel ideas are required to renew the firm and foster growth.

Trilogy of Lessons for Best Practice Long-Term Stewardship

Lesson 1: Value tradition while embracing innovation and change.

Lesson 2: Embrace an LTO as patient owners.

Lesson 3: Good leaders make courageous decisions.

Exemplar Story: Entrepreneurship

In 1980, when the founder of a database tech service company created a name for his business, he used the initial of his last name added to the initials of the first names of his four offspring, aged zero to seven. From the start, he would say, "Look kids, this is a generation-to-generation-to-generation thing. I don't care if you stay in this specific industry, but I do care if you keep your families together the way my father and I kept our families together. That I care about a lot."

The founder had been in his father's business until he started his own. His business ideas were ahead of their time, and part of his challenge was convincing corporations that his firm could do a better job than their in-house operation because of its superior technology, economies of scale, and marketing and other skills. The corporate culture of his business bore the stamp of his forceful personality.

In the late 1990s, the founder established an advisory board that met twice a year. It consisted of the founder, his wife, his four offspring, the company's attorney, the company's accountant, and his college roommate who had served as chief of staff in a U.S. presidential campaign. He used the group as a sounding board and as a vehicle to educate family members about the business.

By 2001, the company had 175 employees in the headquarters and outsourced another 125 to India and the Philippines. It was the biggest player in its niche—40 percent larger than its nearest competitor, with $13 million in annual sales. The recession that year caused the founder to reduce the workforce by 10 percent. He learned a valuable lesson, saying that the prosperous economy before "made us inefficient and allowed lack of discipline. Even with the reduction in force we did not miss a beat in fulfilling our work."

Also in 2001, the elder two of his four children, aged 28 and 25, were working in the business. The two younger ones were in nonbusiness-focused graduate and undergraduate programs, respectively. It was not known whether they would ever join the business. That year, the founder launched a second company using the same technology as in the first, but targeted at two additional industries. The oldest child in the business extended the same technology to a third additional industry, giving that division a new name. The youngest in the business spearheaded a separate company with yet another name to provide e-blasts services.

The offspring in the business wanted to move forward more quickly on one of the newly launched businesses so as not to miss opportunities in the marketplace. Their father differed: "If your product is better than everyone else's, it should not hurt you if it comes out a year or two later." He told them that he would welcome three or four good competitors. "The marketplace is so large there's plenty of business for everybody," he said. "And I'd just as soon not be out there ploughing all this new ground myself, in front of everybody."

One offspring said, "Dad is an entrepreneur at heart, but I think he is getting a little tired. I don't think he wants to go through this whole process of staying here until late at night every night all over again to start this new company. . . . That's really the job of my sibling and me—to take this business to the next level."

The other shared, "My dad's a great marketer, a great salesman. But, even he will say he is not the best manager. I think he's been trying to work on that, but how do you change a fifty-eight-year-old man who's been successful?"

The eldest in the business was currently the vice president of operations. He thought ahead to the future, "I don't think I could run the company. Most of the key executives have known me since I was a kid and I think it will be very difficult for them to accept me as their boss. I have already had to deal with credibility issues." The founder had begun mulling over different ways of choosing a successor other than just appointing one. In some families, he observed, the siblings themselves chose the new leader. Other families were creating an "office of the president," in which siblings became copresidents.

Both children in the business agreed that sooner or later, a restructuring would be necessary. One suggested the creation of a holding company with a top-notch management team and hoped to expand the services into other industries. The other argued that the "family needs to sit down and discuss where everyone needs to be in one, five, and ten years," feeling that it was important to understand the responsibility to oneself and to one's dreams as well as the responsibility to one's family. The founder reflected, "I wanted to try to keep the family together, but if keeping my family together makes their life so onerous, then I've defeated the purpose."

This exemplar story is based on the following case study: John Ward and Elly Andriopoulou, *The Oberman Family and Omeda Communications Inc.*, Kellogg Case #5-105-003, published 2006.

Stewart's Takeaways from the Exemplar Story: Entrepreneurship

- *It is never too early for an entrepreneur to think in terms of EO and LTO. From the get-go of the naming of the company, this entrepreneur thought about being in business over generations with his offspring. There is something powerful in daring to have this dream.*

- *The EO is evident in the second generation, who are starting new businesses within the enterprise.*

- *Still, systems need to be in place to help the family members plan for where they want to be as a business and as individuals over a 5- to 10-year time horizon.*

CHAPTER FIVE

Stewardship

Part of our secret for success: the pride of everyone working in a company that has a set of principles that transcends the generations.
—Samuel Curtis Johnson, Jr., Fourth-Generation Leader,
S.C. Johnson & Son

Stewardship is perhaps the most obvious of my four AGES dimensions that differentiate family businesses from their nonfamily counterparts. The importance of stewardship in a family enterprise makes intuitive sense for even the most casual observer, which is probably why it got my attention very early in my journey to better understanding leadership differences. However, and perhaps surprisingly, stewardship was *not* originally positioned for the family business context. After some digging around I discovered that stewardship, the theory, was introduced to examine situations in which executives are motivated to act in the best interests of their owner principals—the executives act as stewards, in other words.

This idea, novel for its time, conflicted with the prevailing conventional wisdom that saw managers as self-interested agents, who must be closely monitored to align their behaviors with those of their owner principals. This view of the world, which has dominated corporate governance conversation for decades, is known as the *agency dilemma*. In this chapter, I will share what I have gleaned about stewardship, why it is vitally important to me as a leader of the family and the business. To achieve this, however, I first have to walk you through another approach, that of agency. Right up front here I will alert you to the fact that it is tough going in parts, but I encourage you to work hard to grasp the concepts, as they really will make a difference in how you see yourselves and the leadership roles with which you are charged.

Stewardship and Agency

To be able to incorporate stewardship into my mind-set, I first had to master the other side of the coin: agency, or what has become known as the principal-agent problem. I did this intentionally, as a fellow family business leader reminded me one day that "as leaders we spend the bulk of our time reducing agency costs." Once I considered what he actually meant by this, I found he was correct.

Therefore, what did he mean exactly? First, let me admit to my bias here: since I took the time to understand agency theory, I unashamedly live by the mantra that agency explains most of what goes on in any organization, whether family-owned or not. Hopefully, by white boarding the development of these ideas I might help you grasp the essence of agency more quickly.

Principals and Agents

The first thing to know is that in a business context, agency theory explains *relationships* between principals (owners) and agents (those whom principals employ to act on their behalf—i.e., managers). Agents are assumed to be motivated to act in their own self-interest, which may not align with the interests of their owner principals. In many managerial situations, in fact, having access to information that their owner principals do not have enables managers to act in their own interests. This information discrepancy is referred to as *information asymmetry*; when managers use this asymmetry to act in ways unaligned with the intentions of their owners, such as taking excessive risk with the organization to improve their own compensation, we have an example of *moral hazard* (think, insider trading). Moreover, a situation when an agent has private information beforehand is known as *adverse selection* (think, nepotism). Directors can also be regarded as managers as they are appointed to make decisions on behalf of owner principals.

Carrots and Sticks

To mitigate the effects of these behaviors, owner principals invest in "sticks" (punishments) and "carrots" (rewards). Some owners favor carrots and offer *equity shares or options,* for example, to incentivize managers to achieve outcomes the owners value. In addition, most will seek to deter aberrant behavior by investment in sticks such as *monitoring systems* that include internal and external audits and management control systems. Investment in these systems represents real costs to align managerial behavior with owners' intentions. But notwithstanding these various sticks and carrots, there is never perfect alignment between owners and managers; therefore, there will always be some *residual loss*.

When Owners Are Managers

However, the principal-agent dynamics in family businesses are fundamentally different from those of nonfamily firms. In many, if not the majority, of small family firms, the owners *are* the managers. Therefore, by definition misalignment of objectives does not occur, nor does information asymmetry. Moral hazards are avoided. This led early commentators to suggest that family firms have insignificant agency costs because of this natural alignment between owners' and managers' roles. These lower agency costs have been identified as a source of competitive advantage for family firms.

In cases where owners are the managers, it can be assumed that the convergence of ownership and management ensures that information regarding the firm's resources, risk orientation, and growth prospects is shared, or symmetrical. In other words, information asymmetry is reduced. Subsequently, the firm's resources are not misallocated, and monitoring and transaction costs are minimized. But this, from my experience, needs to be interpreted carefully.

While it is clear that family firms have the potential to incur lower agency costs when the goals of owners and managers are closely aligned, it doesn't always happen this way. In fact, family firms can create their own unique types of agency costs, based on their distinctive circumstances. Curiously, I discovered that these costs arise from what we regard as benefits—but benefits that have gotten out of balance. Superficially, these costs come when the alignment of goals referred to earlier becomes "unstuck." Typically, this occurs when incumbent leaders stay for too long and/or we allow our commitment to family to get in the way of smart business decisions. When I investigated these issues I learned they are referred to as *entrenchment* and *altruism*, respectively.

Consider briefly the principal-agent situation as it applies to my context. The founder, my grandfather, would have had limited potential for agency costs as he certainly was the owner and manager, very hands on. My father as the leader of the second generation grew the business and was not able to manage as his father had. He did open himself up to the potential for agency costs but, from my observation, minimized this by building very close relationships with his managers and treating them well. On my watch, I have been very conscious to introduce governance mechanisms to reduce the potential for agency costs. As the business and the family have grown, the potential for information asymmetry, adverse selection (in the business and the family), and altruism have increased significantly.

For me, this behavioral economics perspective provides the insightful framework of ideas on these aforementioned issues. Behavioral economists suggest that individuals (or, in the case of family firms, the dominant family coalition) are motivated by an idiosyncratic set of preferences that may be economic or noneconomic in character; moreover, they may be egoistic or altruistic. Conflicts of interest arise because resource constraints prevent the dominant family coalition from maximizing its different type of preferences simultaneously. In other words, the presence of noneconomic objectives results in the difficulty of aligning various noneconomic objectives of owners and thus cannot guarantee the alignment of owners' attitudes and risk tolerance toward growth opportunities. Paradoxically, this situation is compounded by the informal relationships and governance that often prevail, which reduces the formal safeguards that mitigate such potential agency costs. The effects of these agency costs are more severe on minority, especially nonfamily, shareholders. The dominant family coalition has the power and incentive to act in its own interests, at the expense of outside shareholders.

Entrenchment

A manifestation of this arises in family firms with what has become known as *executive entrenchment* (see definition presented earlier) and its subsequent agency problems. Entrenchment arises from the disproportionate power awarded to the family management, stemming from personalistic familial sources. Although executive entrenchment is not exclusive to family businesses, it is more prevalent in family firms. Entrenchment issues that arise from family relational contracting are likely to increase agency costs because of the tendency of family firms to decouple the family agent's employment from performance and employment risk. This is because a relational contract between the family and family agent involves a set of mutual expectations that are more likely to be based on the family's noneconomic goals and their residual effects (e.g., emotions and sentiments) than nonfamily contracting would likely be. In short, family bonds engender agency contracts that are prone to depart from economic rationality.

The presence of a dominant family group that allows emotions and relationships to color perceptions of competence of executives makes entrenchment more prevalent in family firms. The agency problems resulting from entrenched management are common among family firms that use pyramid cross-holdings to separate ownership from control. Examples of how executives legitimize their entrenchment include hiding or obscuring negative performance, hiring consultants to legitimize decisions, manipulating biased information in self-service, and embarking on business strategies that capitalize on the managers' idiosyncratic skills and abilities, thus making them irreplaceable. Doubtless, we have all seen examples of this in our own firms.

Entrenchment may also lead to significant agency costs in the form of *hold-up problems*. Hold-up occurs when family management, who acquire a disproportionate amount of power based on their family status rather than their skills, impose their self-interest onto the firm by holding the owners hostage. Thus, entrenched family executives in the firm can make both inside and possibly outside directors beholden to them. This situation threatens the board's autonomy and undermines the effectiveness of its oversight role. Eventually, agency costs arise when family CEOs remain in office long after they have ceased to be effective, thus harming firm performance.

Further, strengthening the rights, influence, and power of family management reinforces a vicious cycle promoting further entrenchment, with negative impact on shareholders' overall welfare. Entrenched family members are capable of redistributing benefits to themselves through excessive compensation or special dividends that may adversely affect employee morale and productivity. Examples of moral hazard problems that arise from entrenchment include but are not limited to

1. management's emphasis on short-term profit over long-term goals,
2. reluctance to innovate,
3. pursuing pet projects that enhance the focal executive's image,
4. focus on sales maximization at the expense of profits (also known as "empire-building"), and
5. consumption of executive perquisites and hubris.

Entrenchment can also exacerbate *altruism* and *adverse selection* problems in family firms. Often defined as selflessness, altruism is the principle or practice of concern for the welfare of others. In our family business context there is a tendency, if not properly understood for altruism, to

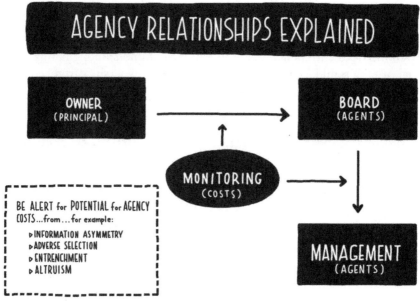

White Board Illustration 5.1. Agency Concept Capture

contribute to agency costs. Consider the example of an entrenched leader who has the authority to reward family members equally, no matter their contribution. Adverse selection can also lead to agency costs because of the limited executive career opportunities available to outsiders; that is, family firms are likely to maintain top management positions for family members rather than hiring more qualified or competent outsiders. Adverse selection results from a smaller pool of labor market of uncertain quality and is most severe in high R&D industries.

I have displayed these concepts in White Board Illustration 5.1.

The Benefit of Agents Who Are Stewards

This basic understanding of agency has made it easier for me to comprehend the importance of stewardship; that's why I consider the concept fundamental to the family business leader's mind-set. I now look at it like this: agents (i.e., those whom principals appoint to work on their behalf) who are stewards gain greater long-term utility from prosocial and collectivist behaviors than from economic, individualist, and self-serving behaviors. When faced with a self-serving decision versus a more cooperative, pro-organizational option, stewards will pursue the latter because of the greater utility they assign to such behaviors. In other words, they give more than they take because they are motivated by a different set of metrics (e.g., continuity). Furthermore, these relationship-centered collaborations within organizations facilitate pro-organizational behaviors and engender trust.

One of the reasons I like stewardship is, and you will note that this is not dissimilar to the EO I framed earlier, that it is divided into subdimensions. There are three psychological dimensions that define and differentiate stewardship from agency theory:

1. Intrinsic motivation
2. Identification with the organization
3. Use of power

I will focus on these in a later chapter that examines individual (rather than organizational) level conversations. But just to whet your appetite, at the individual level a stewardship theoretical perspective focuses on intrinsic needs, which include the desire for personal growth and achievement, affiliation, and self-actualization.

In an effort to gain these higher-order needs, stewards are motivated to work harder on behalf of the organization, which aligns their behaviors with the interests of their principals. In these environments, the potential for opportunism is reduced because agents gain little or no utility by pursuing tangible, self-serving economic rewards. Thus, the more value individual agents place on intrinsic rewards, the less likely they will deviate from the interests of the organization. Conversely, individual agents who are extrinsically motivated will place greater value on tangible rewards. Such circumstances increase monitoring requirements, which form the basis of control within agency theory, and drive agency-related costs. But enough of the individual level for now; let's move on to the organizational level, which makes up one of the cornerstones of my AGES framework and thinking.

Stewardship at the Organizational Level

The authors who first introduced stewardship, the theory, into our rhetoric, as well as the concept of the individual (psychological) level, also identified three key organizational (situational) factors:

1. The extent to which the organization values collectivism over individualism
2. The level of power distance accepted within the ranks of employees
3. Involvement orientation

STEWARDSHIP *redefined*

PSYCHOLOGICAL (INDIVIDUAL LEVEL)	**SITUATIONAL** (ORGANIZATION LEVEL)
1. INTRINSIC (rather than extrinsic) MOTIVATION	**1.** COLLECTIVIST CULTURE (rather than individualism)
2. (HIGH) ORGANIZATIONAL IDENTIFICATION	**2.** LOW POWER DISTANCE
3. USE PERSONAL (rather than POSITIONAL) FORMS of POWER	**3.** INVOLVEMENT ORIENTATION

White Board Illustration 5.2. Stewardship Redefined

I have shown this in White Board Illustration 5.2.

Stewardship is characterized by the extent to which an organization adopts a *collectivist* rather than an individualist culture. And this certainly resonates for family firms. An individualist culture is one in which the attainment of personal goals and objectives is prized. In these cultures, exchanges are evaluated on a short-term basis and are usually viewed in the context of economic cost–benefit analyses. In contrast, collectivist cultures are characterized by group identity, a sense of belonging, and an emphasis on the accomplishment of organizational goals. People in collectivist cultures define themselves as part of the organization. These words ring so true for family businesses, and it should be obvious why stewardship attracted my attention. But there's more.

Power distance, or the extent to which less powerful members of an organization accept unequal distribution of power across levels of the organization, is another pillar of stewardship. In high-power-distance organizational cultures,

1. people with less power are dependent on those with greater power,
2. status and special privileges are given to those with higher rank, and
3. obedience and respect for those of rank are fostered.

In contrast, low-power-distance organizational cultures are those in which interactions are egalitarian, inequalities are discouraged, and organizational members are treated equally. The fundamental argument is that a stewardship orientation is identifiable through the promotion of equality and alignment among the rights and privileges of principals and individual agents, or the characteristics of low power distance. Again, it is clear to see what I was drawn to here.

The final subdimension of the organizational level concerns the degree to which there is an *involvement orientation*. This view fosters a work climate of self-control and self-management in which employees are challenged with the responsibility to develop new ideas and new approaches to solve organizational problems. Or, put another way, an involvement-oriented management environment is one in which people are allowed and empowered to reach their full potential.

An Illustrative Case

To bring these stewardship concepts at the organizational level (*collectivist culture, power distance,* and *involvement*) to life, I would like to share a story of a family that was able to navigate a near-death situation due to their being stewardship dimensions in place. Specifically, the case of the DeMoulas Family in New England. I along with many others followed this modern-day Shakespearean-like drama in the media. I was so fascinated that I approached a Boston professor to commission a group of his MBA students to document the proceedings. The following is their capture, with my edits interwoven.

Market Basket

Market Basket, a subsidiary of DeMoulas Super Markets, Inc., is a New England institution providing low-cost, high-quality groceries across Massachusetts, New Hampshire, and Maine. Headquartered in Tewksbury, Massachusetts, this chain of supermarkets operating in the *Supermarkets and Other Grocery (Except Convenience) Stores* industry operates 73 individual stores across the region. Table 5.1 provides the summary details of the company and the family since founding in 1917.

As can be seen, under Mike's and then his son Arthur T. DeMoulas's (Arthur T.) leadership, Market Basket grew from a small neighborhood shop into a $4 billion conglomerate. During its ascendance, Market Basket maintained its community ties, especially while Arthur T. served as CEO. During his tenure, Arthur T. promoted efforts closely aligned with the stewardship dimensions of *collectivist culture, low power distance,*

Table 5.1 Market Basket, Timeline of Significant Events

Year	Significant Event
1917	The grocery chain had its origin in a neighborhood food store in Lowell that was opened in 1917 by Greek immigrants Arthur and his wife Efrasine DeMoulas.
1938	Bank threatens to foreclose if a $100 payment was not made; the family was able to raise the money to keep the business afloat as their son Telemachus "Mike" left school to work at the store.
1954	Eldest son George returned from the army and also joined the family business. Within 15 years, the two brothers help transform the mom and pop–style store into a more modern supermarket chain consisting of 15 stores with sales of $900,000.
	The founders sell the business to two of their six children, George and Telemachus.
1964	Mike and George, along with their wives, met at the office to sign the wills of one another, in which each was named executor of the other's estate. During this meeting, it has been reported that Mike and George made a verbal agreement that whichever of the brothers lived longer would care for the other's family and that the family wealth would be divided evenly among the two sides of the family.
1971	George DeMoulas died suddenly on June 27, 1971, while vacationing with his family in Greece. On George's death, Telemachus DeMoulas took control. Evanthea (wife of George) acquired half of the shares and along with her son, Evan, were given seats on the board of directors; they let Mike handle all of the paperwork given he was trusted as the patriarch of the family. After George's death, as his children were young, and even in later years, his family relied totally on Mike and developed little business sense of their own. Mike oversaw the operations of the DeMoulas supermarkets while also opening a new chain of stores, what is known today as "Market Basket," as a way, according to Mike, to get around a Massachusetts law that limited the number of liquor licenses that could be held by one supermarket chain.
1980	Mike had Evanthea removed from the board of directors, saying she was unsuitable to serve after it was discovered she was carrying on an affair with a married man. Over the course of many years after George's death, Mike transferred many of George's shares into his name and later moved the assets to his side of the family and into the Market Basket stores. Amazingly this activity started around six weeks after George's death in 1971.

1990	The family feud over control of the company burst onto the public scene in 1990, when Arthur S. DeMoulas, a son of George, filed a complaint that Telemachus DeMoulas was diverting assets from the chain into businesses solely owned by his branch of the family. After one of the longest, costliest, and nastiest court battles in the state's legal history, Telemachus DeMoulas was eventually forced to pay George's relatives $206 million. The judge awarded 50.5 percent of the shares, a controlling interest, to George's heirs.
2008	George's daughter-in-law Rafaela votes in favor of Telemachus's son, Arthur T., in a board election. Arthur T. is made president of the business.
2013	Rafaela switches her vote, giving Arthur S. control of the board.
2014 (summer)	At Arthur S.'s urging, board fires Arthur T., replacing him with co-CEOs Felicia Thornton and James Gooch. Employees and their supporters, including loyal customers, rallied at Market Basket's corporate headquarters urging his reinstatement. The fight involved nearly the entire 25,000-person workforce, from cashiers to store managers.
2014 (fall)	Arthur T. DeMoulas offers to buy the 50.5 percent share controlled by opposing relatives to regain control of the fractured company.

and *genuine involvement* with the organization. Arthur T. displayed a tremendous amount of understanding of the importance of nurturing a stewardship orientation. By investing company resources in programs to improve their lives and sharing some of the value created by the business, he consciously reduced agency-related costs.

Arthur T. was fired in March 2014 by his cousin, Arthur S. DeMoulas (Arthur S.), chairman of Market Basket's board of directors, who accused him of reckless spending of the company's resources, and business deals favorable to his side of the family. Arthur S. had a distinctly different approach to the business than Arthur T. Think the inverse of stewardship dimensions. Rather than invest in the community, Arthur S.'s focus was to increase returns to shareholders; between 2001 and 2011 Arthur S.'s side of the family received $425 million in dividends. Soon after Arthur T.'s firing, Arthur S. appointed co-CEOs, both from outside the family and the grocery industry, to run Market Basket.

Interestingly, the benevolence Arthur T. had shown toward the community was quickly reciprocated. After several rallies and escalating calls for Arthur T.'s return fell on deaf ears, many longtime employees loyal to Arthur T., particularly in operations and logistics, staged a walkout, effectively shutting down the company's supply chain for 41 days.

During this time, the Market Basket stores remained open but quickly ran out of perishable goods and slowly ran out of other goods. Many longtime customers also boycotted the chain in response to the situation. After much wrangling and discussion, the company's employees, suppliers, and customers were ultimately victorious, with Arthur S.'s faction forced to accept a buyout offer and relinquish control of the paralyzed company back to Arthur T. As soon as Arthur T. regained control and was reinstated, almost all of the employees, suppliers, and customers came rushing back, and Market Basket was back in business in short order.

Linking the DeMoulas family situation back to the concept of agency and stewardship, I suggest Arthur T.'s behavior to be consistent with many of the dimensions of stewardship. Indeed, by seeing the community as pivotal to the business and appreciating the importance of maintaining relationships with members of the communities in which Market Basket operates with a heightened level of benevolence, Market Basket's interests are properly balanced.

Further evidence of the significant "value" for the concepts captured by pursuing a stewardship orientation can be established vis-à-vis the final chapter of the saga. On August 27, 2014, Arthur T.'s side of the family agreed to buy out their cousins' stake in the company for more than $1.5 billion, implicitly valuing the company at over $3 billion, or about 13.8 times 2013 earnings, which is on the low end of publicly traded grocery store valuations, with P/E ratios that range from 9.8 to 38.2,[1] suggesting that Arthur T.'s side got a relatively good deal, which is not surprising considering that without him the chain effectively shut down.

Another Market Basket Story Takeaway

While here I have employed the DeMoulas family to illustrate stewardship, my deeper purpose is to also highlight something that I genuinely believe: specifically that family businesses are concerned with generating economic and noneconomic wealth, which means that their owners are committed to the long-term interests of the firm, and are therefore likely to make decisions using not just using an economic calculus but also a moral/social calculus in order to ensure the firm's survival. That can happen only through an ongoing partnership with the society in which the business operates. Warning: this is where I get on my soap box. I believe *all* businesses should be operated with an eye on economic and noneconomic issues (as family businesses tend to do).

The message I take from the Market Basket case and the DeMoulas family saga is that I need to learn from family situations that go awry. While seeking aspirational families to learn from I also seek out situations (and there are many) where families have not been able to manage the complexities of continuity. In this instance I relied on secondary sources of information, and certainly there is more to the story than I was privy to. But the message should be clear: reducing the potential for agency costs whether in the family or the business is a leader's priority, and promoting a stewardship climate is one way to address this. Put another way, it's critical to understand agency and stewardship fully!

Summary

Promoting stewardship within your organization has clear economic and noneconomic advantages. But to genuinely understand stewardship, it is important, I think, to be comfortable with the concepts canvased in agency theory. Particularly relevant to our family business leader situation are the roles played by entrenchment, altruism, and adverse selection. While not unique to our context, once understood, I suggest these are useful in better considering how the aforementioned architecture initiatives are designed in order to effectively reduce the potential for unnecessary (agency-related) costs. To support the importance of stewardship in my AGES framework, I really like the work of Miller and Le Breton-Miller (2005), who characterize stewardship as having three main priorities: continuity of the business, community of employees, and connection with customers. The Market Basket story, I think, reinforces this.

Trilogy of Lessons for Best Practice Long-Term Stewardship

Lesson 1: Focus to build multigenerational legacy.

Lesson 2: Accept the responsibility of long-term social and economic value creation.

Lesson 3: Embrace the obligation to generate returns to a wider group of stakeholders.

Exemplar Story: Stewardship

In 2009, an eldest son became G2 president of his Family Fastener Firm (FFF), the company his father had purchased 30 years earlier and built into a $50 million business. By 2012, the firm had become a true family enterprise, with all three members of the second generation involved in the business while their father remained in his roles as CEO and board chair. Between the three years, the G2 president had led the company out of U.S. recession and through a major acquisition, further developing his own leadership style while managing relationships with his executive team, his father, and his siblings. Revenues had grown to $78 million.

Now that all three offspring were part of the business, the eldest found himself to be a coach for his younger siblings, appreciating their openness to his input and willingness to challenge his ideas and decisions. Their discussions also led to valuable feedback that the president could share with his management team. At the same time, the G2 president consciously balanced guidance with humility and support in dealing with his relatives as they progressed within the company.

The president believed his father had run the company with "his heart and his gut" but that it was best for him to use his "heart and his head." He shared characteristics with his father (i.e., a caring approach to customers and employees) while incorporating his own personal approach (i.e., more analytical) that he thought helped him and the company make a smoother leadership transition.

In line with this, he was viewed by the management team as being more of a "professional manager," focused on empowering those who reported to him and at times deferring to them on key decisions. He took a strong interest in personal career development of employees and put several performance measures in place, along with reporting on personal development at board meetings and working with the company's HR department on development-focused surveys. He wanted to establish employee development as a pillar of the company's culture.

The president espoused a leadership philosophy based on the notion of "servant leadership," making it a top priority to serve the teams and organization in order to keep morale and performance high. A central tenet of this approach was that leadership is much more about the journey than the destination. "It's about personal integrity," reflected the president. "If you're trying to be one person in one place and a different person in another, that won't work, especially in a family business. If you don't believe in your approach, people will see right through it."

A natural extension of this mind-set was that the whole of the business and family is larger than any one part or individual. Embracing that concept allows servant leaders to put aside their own self-interest for the good of the family and/or business. The president believed this leadership approach fit more naturally in family business, where it is easier to see the importance of the collective good.

The president implemented four pillars of the FFF way:

1. Practice servant leadership (humility). All employees rolling up their collective sleeves, with no task beneath anyone. For example, everyone was responsible for looking out for others at FFF and for pitching in to make sure the office and plant were clean.

2. Same-day response (dedication). Urgency around communications so as not to leave any internal or external customer waiting for answers to questions. True dedication required this kind of vigilance.

3. Speak the truth (integrity). Transparency in company communications, such as financial reporting, and interpersonal interactions. "It's about being the same person when we walk in the door to the office as we are when we walk through the door at home," he said.

4. Go the extra mile (passion). Doing something for a customer or colleague that was unexpected and thoughtful.

Of himself, he said, "I strive for personal alignment. It's about having 360 degrees of accountability not only to the management team and board, but to the family, as well. I have to be true to myself and blend that with what works for the family and the business. It's important to view the family business as a gift and to truly appreciate it."

This exemplar story is based on the following case study: John Ward, Brent C. Stern, Carol Adler Zsolnay, and Sachin Waikar, *ATF, Inc.: Fasteners and Family,* Kellogg Case #5-113-004, published 2016.

Stewart's Takeaways from the Exemplar Story: Stewardship

*   Stewardship can be institutionalized, rather than just existing at the individual level.

*   Areas of stewardship include the personal, employee, and organizational levels.

*   A stewardship approach to leadership can turn into a stewardship approach to how a business operates toward all of its constituents.

Note

1. Fulcrum. 2015. Valuation guide: Grocery stores. Retrieved from http://www.fulcrum.com/grocerystores_appraisal/.

CHAPTER SIX

Learning Leadership Roles

If you don't occasionally make a mistake, you aren't trying hard enough.
>—Arthur Ochs Sulzberger, Jr., Fourth-Generation Leader,
>*The New York Times* Company

Over the years I have noticed how family business leaders develop and display their skillsets and mind-sets when *preparing* to take on their roles, *enacting* them, and *exiting* them. It seems to me that their mind-set then often affects what skills they deem important or not so important. Furthermore, their mind-set can be influenced by their preparation for their leadership role. Families, I have spoken with, that tend to stress learning, for example, often build stronger capabilities among their family's human resources. This learning is optimized when it starts early and accompanies the leader through his or her development. In this chapter I introduce the *4Ls Framework*, which positions leaders' development through four phases (White Board Illustration 6.1):

1. Learning business (L1)
2. Learning our business (L2)
3. Learning to lead our business (L3)
4. Learning to let go (L4)

For each of the four discrete learning *phases*, I will include a learning *priority*, a specific *paradox* for each learning priority, and the specific *pathways* successful firms have developed to manage each learning phase's paradox in accordance with its learning priority.

White Board Illustration 6.1. The 4Ls Framework

L1: Learning Business

All leaders must learn the fundamental skills of managing a business. Many of these skills are common to all businesses, whatever their form of ownership. But the family firm faces specific issues requiring leaders to go beyond merely knowing what stage the firm has reached in its organizational life cycle. Leaders need to recognize not only that managing a family-owned business requires some unique knowledge and skills but also that the process of learning these will itself be different than in a nonfamily business.

Learning what it takes to be involved in a family business requires *prioritizing* learning personal management, particularly the *self-discipline* that business leadership requires. People skills are also vital. Technical skills of business are of lesser importance but not to be overlooked. I am of the belief that the fundamental general business skills future leaders need are the following:

- Self-management skills
- People skills
- Practical knowledge
- Ongoing learning
- Creativity

Should these skills be learned inside or outside the family firm? I'm often asked this question. This "inside–outside" dimension regarding learning basic business knowledge is at the heart of the first *paradox* I discovered on my own family business learning journey. A good analogy is the biblical parable of the Prodigal Son, who leaves his father's house and eventually returns, but only after disappearing for a long time, wasting his inheritance, and being virtually given up for lost. In a similar way, "going outside" in order to "return inside" the firm is both a vital opportunity for learning and a potential threat to the family nature of the business.

It is vital to learning because the younger generation needs to develop skills and gain perspectives they cannot acquire at the same breadth or depth by staying in the family business. Rising family members also need to prove themselves worthy of a place in the senior management structure of the firm and can do so by excelling outside of it. But going outside is also a threat to the survival of the firm *as a family firm* because the person who leaves the family business setting to learn about how to run a business may choose not to return.

Despite this trade-off, there seems to be only one viable *pathway* through the inside–outside paradox: "go outside anyway"; that is, it is generally accepted that future managers of family-owned businesses must leave that business at an early career stage so that they are better equipped to serve the firm later. My leadership contacts recommend this course of action, usually for an extended period, regardless of the organizational life cycle stage the family firm is in. Nevertheless, the stage of the family firm in terms of the business life cycle affects the relevance of the *location* where the outside experience is gained. For example, if the family firm is moving toward maturity, then outside experience and learning that assists the family firm to make that transition is highly beneficial.

Dealing with the necessity to leave the family firm has a number of consequences for family business members, such as the need to accept uncertainty and to keep the route back to the family firm open.

L2: Learning *Our* Business

Learners returning to the family firm after gaining outside experience typically do more than simply continue the same kind of learning. Working in the family firm entails learning *our* business. At first glance, you might think that this would be like coming to grips with the specific issues associated with any business, but there is certainly more to it than that.

Learning our business has to do with *prioritizing* the understanding and valuing the values of that business and the values of the people who had been—and often still are—associated with creating it. Getting this critical learning right ultimately prepares the learner to lead the family business.

My experience has certainly been that learning our business is different from learning business in general. What is it about our business that seemed to be of special value? This brings up yet another *paradox*. This one arises from the question of how you maintain a sense of sameness, of continuity, that enables owners and customers alike to see the business as "the same" family business while it is dealing with a rapidly changing world by evolving accordingly.

I certainly learned from the older generation even before joining the firm. In particular, I learned the value of capacity for hard work and determination from my father and grandpa. I also learned from my father the need to admit when I made a mistake, which, as it turns out, is often.

Moreover, continuing with the traditions of the past was indeed a feature of my learning. An area that frequently exemplified continuity of values was our family's use of debt. The prevailing conventional wisdom of academic researchers and family business consultants alike is that family businesses are typically not interested in sharing ownership with shareholders outside the family because their financial policies generally minimize the risk of losing independence. This is seen in their preference for retained earnings or bank loans over outside equity finance to fund growth. This has been described as family firms' "strategic conservatism," a term I can certainly identify with, based on my experience with our business and values.

The use of debt in family firms reflects the *paradox* that comes with learning *our* business. Learning our business means getting beyond the general skills learned in the first stage (learning business) and appreciating what is special about *this* business. As a family business, this means "perpetuating values." In short, a particular set of values—business values and personal values—are there to be learned, cherished, and passed on. But because the growth needs of the firm change with its position on the life cycle curve, the values are likely to be "continued differently"; that is, the values of the family business—including a basically conservative approach to debt—are absorbed so that the learner feels that he or she is part of something special about *our* business: because our values are special, because they add something, they should be continued. But this is not to say that everything should be done in exactly the same way as the preceding generation would have done it.

A founder's values and belief system can be an anchor allowing the incorporation of new learning over time as an organization interacts with the world at large. More recently others have suggested that retaining a connectedness to the past and simultaneously adapting and living the founder's vision is a tremendous and underexploited asset in family firms. Beyond excellent management and governance, true sustenance for multigenerational family firms requires a self-sustaining, self-regulated family organization to assure that a unique culture of values and meaning provide motivations beyond money.

In general, family enterprise leaders need to learn that the businesses they lead have a more important element of *tradition* than most corporations do. It is extremely important, on the one hand, to respect traditions because they are an integral element of family companies. On the other, it's also critical to vary the business practices arising from traditions to ensure the continuity of the business.

Therefore in learning *our* business and its values, I adhere to the notion that we are "the same, only different" from other businesses. Looking back, I now can appreciate taking the time to learn and maintain the broad management philosophy of the previous generation, rather than the specific detail of their strategies. The pathway I pursue to manage this paradox, which seems particular to family businesses, is to value values and continuing them on my watch, while also being conscious that I need to continue them *differently*. My journey to leadership also required me to learn about the market value of being a family firm, which in many ways was the genesis of this book.

L3: Learning to Lead

The 4Ls Framework moves from learning about business and about *our* business to learning about being *in charge* of the family-owned business, or enacting leadership. Thus, the next learning stage is learning to *lead* our business. This suggests some new questions: what is leadership and what might be special about how future owner-managers of family businesses learn it? Much research has been done into different types or styles of leadership. But how do these relate to the stage the business has reached in its life cycle and how do they relate to family business?

Ideas for leading family business are often gained by working outside the business and by constantly scanning the environment. Values, by contrast, are learned *inside* the business from the family itself and by applying knowledge gained outside to the special situation and particular qualities of the family business. This, of course, is no small task. Therefore what qualities of perspicacity on the part of the leader are required to bring these two systems—family and business—together for the benefit of both?

Judging the needs of the business alone in terms of the business life cycle also requires qualities of perspicacity. The changes in development denoted by the business life cycle suggest that the distinction between *transactional* and *transformational* leadership is likely to be relevant to family business, just as it is to others. Consistent with the more general literature on transactional and transformational leadership, it seems likely that transactional leadership in family business will be appropriate for handling the transactions relevant to the current stage of the organizational life cycle, whatever that may be for a given enterprise. Transformational approaches, on the other hand, would be needed if the family business leader judges that he or she needs to guide it through a transition to a more developed stage on the life cycle curve.

Achieving the insight needed to lead the family firm is a *priority* in this phase, as it often seems to center on knowing how to use apparently contradictory management-control approaches simultaneously. Paralleling this, the notion of "informal formality" is part of the territory—that is, the exercising of formal and informal controls together—certainly *paradoxical*.

To be sure, there is no obvious *pathway* through the problem of leading a family business, as I've learned firsthand. Rather than a simple choice, leadership turns out to be a careful balance between ostensibly opposing approaches. As family firms professionalize, their leaders typically introduce outsiders, formal boards, complex information-gathering systems, and other control devices that bring greater formality and potential for wider participation in decision making. The *pathway*, therefore, involves leading the family and firm through the determination of strategy, structure, and systems, that is, architecture.

In this context, attending to business needs in ways that respect the legitimate interests of all family and business stakeholders will entail mastering five key learning tasks:

1. Managers of family firms should adopt management systems adequate for the demands of their external and internal environments, as well as for their firm's development stage.
2. Management approaches should form an internally consistent architecture package of strategies, structures, and systems.
3. Management systems must evolve dynamically as the business grows and matures.
4. Professionalism in management is vital for systems development.
5. The absence of succession plans will seriously inhibit professionalization of the firm.

Part of this professionalization process, which represents another way in which leaders achieve perspicacity or insight as the firm moves along the organizational life cycle curve, is to make greater use of formal control through directors' meetings. Even with the operations of the board, a kind of informal formality tends to be maintained in family business, as one leader pointed out when discussing how he had pushed the firm in a more market-oriented direction:

> One of the changes [associated with firm's move towards a greater market focus] was to change the board structure. We have never operated an efficient board, and may never do so, in fact. We have a conflict between the roles of the board and the roles of the senior management team. For example, the board spends a large proportion of its time monitoring the performance of the senior management, when the senior management is spending a lot of time monitoring its own performance and the performance of the business—an obvious duplication. Also a lack of ability by the board to think strategically—a lot of strategic decisions are being made by the management.

L4: Learning to Let Go

All organizations undergo transitions as they change, and this is often most noticeable with the appointment of a new CEO, meaning the exit of the previous top leader. Considerable attention has been devoted to the issue of CEO succession in firms in general, typically in the context of publicly owned companies. But privately held family businesses also face succession issues, to such an extent that succession dominates the family research literature. In fact, some say that the three most important issues confronting a family business are "succession, succession, and succession."

But letting go is yet another *paradoxical* leadership problem because it has to do with planning what needs to happen when the incumbent CEO—the one who's currently in place—is no longer there; that is, the incumbent CEO is indeed leading, but in order to let go. A further feature of letting go our business is that, contrary to what the words themselves might suggest, letting go is not so much an event as a *process* of transition. One must, paradoxically, "learn to let go to lead to let go." Let us now examine the stages of letting go the business, and the factors that influence how incumbent family business CEOs learn to handle this process.

Many years ago, scholars identified the CEO exit styles exhibited by family business leaders as representing four distinct types: monarch, general, ambassador, and governor. These mind-sets affect what skills are deemed significant for leaders. Monarchs and generals, especially when approaching what would be regarded as an exit point, tend to focus on *themselves* and not those succeeding them. This self-interested focus tends to undermine any steward-like behavior, especially those reflecting a learning orientation displayed through being a skillful architect and governor. On the other hand, ambassadors and governors are more *steward-like,* as manifest in their display of skills as both architects and governors. Let's take a closer look at each leadership type.

Monarchs have no expectation of early retirement, preferring instead to "die with crowns on." This rule-for-life mind-set tends to ignore the need to think about succession or development of the skillsets of the next generation and often predicts a period of chaos immediately after the monarch's reign ends. While some monarchs have been successful entrepreneurs, their mind-sets are typically not founded on skills that emerge from having been successful architects, governors, or stewards.

Generals leave office reluctantly but plot to return. Their mind-set is thus not one of learning to let go for the next generation of leaders whom they have prepared by developing their skillsets. Instead, a general's plans to return at the expense of "failed" next-generation leaders are best engineered when consequences of their own leadership are inadequate. Typically, generals have not been good architects or governors, and have ignored the need to act as good stewards.

Ambassadors leave by delegating most of their operating responsibilities to next-generation leaders while retaining their "diplomatic" or representational roles. This mind-set is based on a staged exit from the business, enabled by the incumbent leader's development of the next generation's skillset. As such, ambassadors tend to display strong architect and governor skillsets during their leadership.

Governors are those who exit their leadership role according to set departure dates that have been made public. Because of the fixed-term nature of governors' role, planning pervades their leadership. Not surprisingly, governors demonstrate skills that highlight their capabilities as architects to complement their governing capacities. Furthermore, their fixed term promotes a mind-set that exemplifies stewardship.

The process of leaving our business makes the succession process appear logical even if the problem itself is a paradox: "leading in order to let go." However, according to many I have spoken to, just because a process is logical doesn't mean it will be easy. While new leaders can be catalysts for change, factors at the individual and the firm level can make changes messy and difficult, and this is definitely true of succession. As a result, sometimes succession, or any kind of change, may be aborted altogether. Similarly, the continuing presence of "retired" CEOs who have not accepted their new status and found a new role will extend the succession process indefinitely and make it much more difficult. In short, CEOs must be able to become willing outcasts, ideally even welcoming displacement by their own anointed heir.

It follows that heirs, who are typically already active and capably involved in the business, perhaps through a long-standing mentoring process, are essential to the continuation of the enterprise. Well before they move into the top position, they need to be perceived as good performers whom others can trust to lead the business in the future. Equally important is that the designated new CEO be viewed as serious about new strategies or management practices he or she plans to introduce, and to have the expertise to introduce them. Making sure all this happens in a timely and orderly way is in large measure the task of the incumbent CEO as he or she moves from the previously "anointed one" to willing, gracious outcast.

As a result, learning to let go the family business is yet another aspect of the paradoxical qualities of leading, since it requires the leader to plan for when he or she will no longer be leading. The paradox is that where learning the family business in the earlier stages involves learning, achieving, and justifying one's place as the anointed successor, this letting-go stage of learning involves the reverse, or going from established leader to ex-leader. To add to the challenge, most of those I have talked to on this sensitive subject agree it needs to be done *early*— sometimes not much later than the time the CEO first takes over the reins of power. As such, it involves a mental dissociation from the firm that is conscious and deliberate, often just when the firm typically needs the most direct, in-depth involvement of those running it—as it reaches maturity.

Despite this complexity, the *pathways* through the paradox of leading to let go also feature some clarity around tangible tasks. These include planning early for the CEO's retirement, creating management development plans, and making and keeping to a clear plan for the whole process; they likely also include the CEO adopting a future role in the business that, preferably, resembles an "ambassador" or "governor" relationship with the firm.

The best way, I have heard, to inform stakeholders of intent to let go came from a coleader of a second-generation family business. The leader assembled his family and informed them he would be "moving to a 440" and then "to a 330." This was puzzling to all. This very insightful leader went on to explain that he would be working 4 days a week for 40 weeks of the year, and then 3 days a week for 30 weeks of the year, as part of a thoughtful exit plan.

Learning to deal with succession—letting go the family business— shares an important characteristic with the other phases of learning we have discussed. The problem of leaving the business, like the other paradoxes, cannot be made to disappear. The good news is that despite the pattern of increasing management complexity, which is exacerbated when coupled with the problem of family business leadership presents, there are recurring patterns for how successful family businesses have tackled leadership tasks, as informed by the stage the firm has reached in its business life cycle.

Therefore, let's look into some of the approaches that work, sketching the profile of successful family businesses whose leaders have managed the intrinsic paradoxes of linking family and business. At the most basic level, the letting-go *pathway* is simply the following:

- Develop a defined timeline for retirement.
- Create management development systems.
- Stick to the plan.

Succession, Succession, Succession

I suggested early that the topic of succession planning, for a long time, dominated any conversation about family business. After a while, for me, this became tiresome. As my fascination for the complexities of leading a family and a business grew, I found myself gravitating away from succession-related conversations. Yes, it is important and, yes, it is different and, yes, it is difficult. It is different and difficult as one wise pundit pointed out to me because "we are not good at it because we don't do it very often." Indeed, this has become my stock reply when the succession plan topic comes up. The average tenure of our corporate leader contemporaries is three, perhaps five, years. Ours in family business is in the vicinity of 20 years or longer. But the other reason that I grew tired of succession plan conversations is that, in the main, most don't know what it is they are referring to; and I was tired of clarifying.

Succession planning is but one of the multiple types of planning we as family business leaders are charged with, the others being estate/ownership, strategic, and human resource development planning. But this chapter, which connects the AGES framework (organizational level) with the SAGE framework (individual level), is probably a good a place as any to touch on the subject of succession. I stress it will be brief because there is an abundance of material on this topic already out there.

Succession planning typically concerns replacing the leader/manager of the family business, the CEO. Some go further to think about who will own the business when the current owners are gone: succession of ownership. But transitions from one generation to another require succession in seven areas, not just those two. Any program for succession must encompass the following considerations:

1. Values: continuing differently
2. Knowledge: theoretical to practical
3. Relationships: networks
4. Management: micro to macro
5. Authority: cost/revenue center to profit center
6. Leadership: operational management to strategic insight
7. Ownership: technical to emotional

In Table 6.1, I have mapped the what, how, and when for each of these stages. Just because I said I didn't chat about it much doesn't mean I haven't thought about it a *lot*!

Table 6.1 Succession Stages

Stages	What	How	When
Values	Successor demonstrates values congruent with those of owning family	Communicate and educate • Schedule family meetings to agree on values and to share a vision • Reinforce family values, as family values are the foundation of your competitive advantage • Signal consistently that a role in the business is *an* option; *not the only* option	• Now never too soon to commence conversations
Knowledge	Successor transitions from theoretical to practical knowledge with patience and mentoring by incumbent	Plan the "apprenticeship" to extend over five to seven years • Require that next generation members to work outside for three to five years and demonstrate competence by being considered for promotion(s) • Potential successors to appreciate there are challenges but business also provides some precious opportunities	• After an agreed period of working outside the family business • Intentionally equip the next generation with the appropriate knowledge, skills, and abilities as the challenges that they will need to address are different from the ones that the current generation navigated
Relationships	Incumbent turns over key relationships to successor	Introduce key internal and external stakeholders • Introduces stakeholders, including suppliers, customers, and bankers • Expect difficult times; support each other through open and honest communication	• Progressively throughout the apprenticeship phase

Management	Successor moves beyond a focus on micro-dimensions of managing operations to strategic considerations of where the family firm is headed	Clarify roles • Ensure family members have clear roles, with transparent requirements, specified responsibilities, and someone other than a parent to report to, which is remunerated at a level consistent with the role • Involve successors in strategic planning sessions for the business informed by expectations of the owning family	• When business is professionalized with governance structures and processes
Authority	Successor progresses through various levels of managerial responsibility prior to any handover	Design a development career • Progressively delegate (financial) responsibility during mentored apprenticeship	• After having demonstrated "trade-off" decision-making capability
Leadership	Successor develops insight to business, family, and self	Encourage longer-term focus • Intentionally design developmental career that best prepares the next generation for their leadership role • In meetings focus on business, family, and self rather than an exclusive concentration on short-term issues in the business • Document business, financial, and succession plans as the first item on to-do list • Recruit caring constructive critics to assist in the process ensuring you don't procrastinate • In family and business meetings encourage a longer-term focus on business than an exclusive concentration on short-term issues in the business	• Ready, willing, and capable • After governance structures have been established for both business and family

(continued)

Table 6.1 (*continued*)

Stages	What	How	When
Ownership	Incumbent (if able) shares ownership (equity) with next-generation family members	Plan financial security for family and business	• Set a timetable, and stick to it
		• Prepare in advance to be financially secure and not a burden on the business and lead by leaving	
		• Develop financial security through estate planning and retirement plans	
		• Focus on the outcomes you most value	
		• Use professional advisors (accountants, lawyers, and financial planners) to organize the business and plan for these transitions	

Summary

Leading is different in family business versus other types, so it is important to understand that learning to lead is different and more complex in this context as well, as stakeholders are arguably more vested in the preparation for leadership in the family and the business needs to be more intentional around this process. More people are concerned and likely to be asking whether or not they are in good hands, compared to nonfamily business shareholders. Understanding that learning to lead process is necessary but not sufficient. This chapter's purpose was to segue between organizational and individual dimensions, or, more specifically, to frame the individual roles of the steward, the architect, the governor, and the entrepreneur.

Trilogy of Lessons for Best Practice Long-Term Stewardship

Lesson 1: Family leadership requires a learnable skillset.
Lesson 2: Leading by leaving is key to continuity.
Lesson 3: Leadership is a developmental process.

CHAPTER SEVEN

The Steward

> I have to be a steward of the Carlson Companies to continue to earn the support of the rest of the family and our employees who are the key stakeholders. . . . I must work with the family group to insure that they receive economic and psychological value from the company that is equal or better than what they will get in alternative investments.
>
> —Marilyn Carlson Nelson, Second-Generation Leader, Carlson

The concept of stewardship is something that I came across very early in my development as a family business leader. I kept hearing from so-called experts and gurus—and even my father—that I was a "baton holder" charged with taking the baton from the incumbent generation (i.e., him) and handing it on to the next generation (i.e., my children and nieces and nephews). With this explanation came the added piece that I was, in fact, a steward. "How hard could that be?" I said to myself, naïvely. I get to grab hold of this family enterprise thing once all the work has already been done, hang on to it for a while, and then give it over at a predetermined juncture. Indeed, that didn't even seem fair.

As a meaningful aside, though I haven't been able to confirm this, my name (Stewart) was the suggestion of my grandfather, who was hoping that the small enterprise he created would one day be his legacy, and thus by having father name me Stewart he could not so subtly pressure me to *steward* the firm across generations. To be fair, I can confirm that this is why I, in turn, named my firstborn Stewart Jr.!

But in all seriousness, a steward is exactly how I've come to see myself in my role as leader. This is hardly something that is unique to me. Recall that in Chapter 5, I introduced the concept of stewardship at the organizational level (as composed of culture, power, distance, and involvement). Well, as I mentioned briefly, there is more to the story, and this concerns the *individual* aspect of stewardship, in other words, *the* steward. That's what this chapter is about. More specifically, I will focus here on how I see our roles as family business leaders being very much aligned with the individual dimensions of stewardship.

Three Individual Dimensions of Stewardship

Just as at the firm level, I have come to understand that there are three *individual* dimensions to being a steward: motivation, identification, and power. (And the more I learn about this area, the more I find it is common sense—and everyone knows that the thing to know about common sense is that it is not that common!) Let's talk about each dimension.

Motivation

The first dimension refers to *motivation*; the critical idea here is that stewards are *intrinsically* motivated, not extrinsically motivated. In layman's language, this simply means that stewards (i.e., we) are not motivated primarily by "things" we can secure. Rather, we are motivated by the benefits we feel for doing what it is that we do. Now, before I am accused of going all "Kumbaya" on you, this does not imply that those of us in stewardship roles receive no tangible benefits for our contribution. On the contrary, we do receive, and expect, compensation that is competitive; but that's not the exclusive or even primary reason for doing what we do. As a friend said to me when discussing this, the key to being effective is loving what you do. But note that this "loving what you do" concept is not necessarily immediate. While I have met plenty of family business leaders who have told me that "all they ever wanted to do was work with my father," other leaders of family enterprise stress that they were not always enamored of being in their family business and typically reflect that they "learned to love it."

In one instance, when I probed further, the leader shared that his uncle made it very challenging for him to be comfortable in whatever role he undertook in the business. Therefore, when I asked how he resolved this issue, he said quite frankly that first he did the math and convinced himself that he had time on his side: his uncle was not going to be around forever! But the critical thing he did was to prove to his uncle and himself that he actually had the motivation and mettle required to contribute to the business, specifically by knuckling down and concentrating on customer-centered innovation. To do this, he visited as many customers as he could and simply asked them their biggest problem; then, once he genuinely understood their pain, he did something about it. That approach resulted in a product that revolutionized the industry and the company, and set it on a path to market dominance. He not only proved his mettle but certainly learned to love the business in the process. I have rarely met a prouder family business leader. In fact, I had the pleasure of walking through his facility recently, where it became clear how much he loved the business and, more important, how much everyone in the business admired him.

This concept of intrinsic motivation is a distinctive component of what differentiates family business leadership from that of other enterprises. And leadership in this instance is not referring only to the individual leader. As it is intangible, intrinsic motivation is hard to define fully, but by definition it comes from *within*. Further, this complexity of definition makes the concept hard to teach. Like many of the topics I've covered in this book, it can't be taught in business school, for example. As such, the onus is firmly on the family system to disseminate what it means to be part of the business family. I was lucky to "see it" early, but I know there are many others who take longer to understand what it really means to belong to a family in business. If the stated (or implied) intention is to perpetuate your business family status, there needs to be an appreciation of the importance of intrinsic motivation.

Identification with the Business

A second dimension of the individual component of stewardship relates to the *identification* of those involved in the business with the business. In other words, the most effective stewards see the business as an extension of themselves. This again is how I see myself and how many in my position, no doubt, see themselves. As one sixth-generation family leader shared with me one cold rainy day in Boston some years ago: "In my experience, those genuinely serious about a role in their family business don't see it as a job, nor a career; it is more akin to a vocation." In contrast, recall the leader who reminded me that "ability is thicker than blood," reinforcing that increasingly complex businesses require well-equipped leaders for performance and longevity.

Therefore, what does seeing the business as an extension of oneself actually mean, and what are the upsides and downsides of such an approach? This is something that I spend more time thinking about than perhaps I should. My conclusion from observing my situation and those of others is that the downside is that you are always "on" and that means that you face continual challenges separating yourself from anything to do with business. This is a potential issue, especially in the context of family relationships. Regrettably, the divorce courts are littered with those in our community who did not successfully manage the business–family separation. For instance, a very good friend and leader of a third-generation business family was called on to work even harder during the recent recession to save his 90-year-old family business from bankruptcy; he saved the firm but lost his relationship, as when the business finally did turn around there was virtually nothing left of his marriage. It happens.

Power

The third dimension relates to how stewards use *power*; that is, stewards don't rely on positional power to get stakeholders engaged. They (we)

White Board Illustration 7.1. Serving and Leading

are more likely to get things done by using what is known as "personal power." It matters very little whether my title is owner, CEO, or, as one of my colorful contemporaries describes himself, "Chief of Jack"; as a steward I understand that it is *respect* that will get the job done. The biggest fear for me, and I know it was for my father as well, is that the next generation will have a sense of entitlement. Recall the example I mentioned earlier about the heir whose mother reminded him often that he needed to work harder than his fellow workers because, unlike him, they'd earned their jobs.

Increasingly, as my understanding of the family business space grows, I'm reminded that entitlement is my enemy. My father didn't paint it in these exact terms, but on reflection he instilled in me that I needed to earn respect and that though my path was going to be different from his, in many ways it was the same because, like him, I was entitled to an easy road. But something he did stress is that in order to be able to lead I needed to be able to serve, which, as I found out much later, are the tenets of servant leadership (White Board Illustration 7.1).

Servant Leadership

All of this leads me to the critical topic of servant leadership. There are so many adjectives to describe leadership that I'm hesitant to single one out, but this one is worthy of focus as it really (really) resonates with "our" space. The concept of servant leadership, if you look into it with some depth, has theological roots. But several authors have taken the rich spiritual base and contextualized it in the organization. Recently I met a leader of a second-generation family business who shared that since he came across the concept of servant leadership in 1992, he has built his company around it. Note that this is a global company with 2,300 employees, many of whom are truly empowered and most of whom apparently live by the servant leadership philosophies. Notably, his interpretation of long-term orientation (LTO) is captured with the servant leadership notion of *gradualism*. He also shared that he was drawn to the fact that servant leadership requires a tolerance of imperfection, something I could really relate to in my family.

Therefore what are the other central tenets? In its purest form, servant leadership has 11 dimensions. But by now you've probably worked out that I can't grasp something with that many dimensions, so I have found a study that captures servant leadership in five factors. This particular study—methodically sound, by the way—tested the five dimensions rigorously, so I feel confident in sharing their findings here. It's easiest to capture the dimensions in an acronym (and by now you know how much

I love those!): WEAP-S, for wisdom, empathy, altruism, persuasiveness, and stewardship. Noteworthy is the inclusion of stewardship. Each of these five dimensions warrants a brief explanation as the context in which these words are used does matter, as suggested here:

1. *Wisdom:* Servant leaders are observant and anticipatory across multiple contexts, enabling them to appropriately apply their knowledge to forward action.
2. *Empathy (emotional healing):* Servant leaders are highly empathic and are able to show sensitivity to others' concerns.
3. *Altruism:* Servant leaders positively influence through service and desire to promote positive development in individuals, organizations, communities, and societies.
4. *Persuasiveness (persuasive mapping):* Servant leaders high in persuasive mapping are skilled at articulating issues and conceptualizing possibilities that are compelling by sharing their train of thought. They rely on persuasion rather than coercion or manipulation.
5. *Stewardship (organizational):* Servant leaders have a genuine ideology to advocate that their organization creates value for their community.

Something else that has developed alongside my appreciation of stewardship and servant leadership, and which has become one of my favorite topics when thinking about being a steward, relates to Maslow's hierarchy of needs.

Questioning Maslow's Hierarchy

Anyone who's undertaken an introduction course in most any social sciences discipline has been introduced to the concept of Maslow's Hierarchy of Human Needs and its iconic pyramid structure. It is fundamental to how individuals develop and survive. I won't waste time reproducing it at length, but I will suggest that, in the context of family business, it is flawed. Before you slam the book shut and claim I am messing with one of the most fundamental humanistic concepts, let me assure you I have evidence. Like many, I went to college after high school and sat through the obligatory foundation studies, including one that introduced me to Maslow's hierarchy. I can't recall much, but I can recall that I was not convinced about this particular pyramid's validity. I admit that I didn't think much more about it back then; I just passed the exam and deleted the files.

However, for some reason the concepts stuck with me, and not that long ago I white boarded my thoughts (White Board Illustration 7.2). The reason for my conundrum came with my inevitable maturation and associated life experiences. I am now at stage of my life where, according to Maslow, I should be self-actualized. But is that it, Dr. Maslow? Does that mean I now coast for the next 50 years? I scratched my head about this for longer than normal and, as things often happen, stumbled over an answer to my bafflement in a nonrelated source, a book about paradox by Charles Handy: *The Empty Raincoat*. I recommend the work heartily, but indulge me as I share what he says about Maslow's pyramid:

> Maslow was right when he postulated that there was a hierarchy of needs, that when you had enough material goods you moved your sights to social prestige and then to self-realization. Perhaps, however, his hierarchy did not reach far enough. There could be a stage beyond self-realization, a stage which we might call *idealization, the pursuit of an ideal or a cause which is more than oneself.* It is this extra stage which would redeem the self-centered tone of Maslow's thesis which, for all that it rings true of much of our experience, has a rather bitter aftertaste. Maslow himself was to acknowledge this toward the end of his life. (emphasis mine)

Enough said on that topic. I'll leave it to you to consider its meaning for you, depending on where you are in your life stage. But, often now, I find myself pondering the implications of the hierarchy for leaders of business families.

Intrinsic Motivation, Proximal Goals

Handy's reference earlier to the concept of ideals in the context of how we behave generally and, more specifically, as leaders piqued my interest and led me on another inquisitive journey. While seeking to better understand behavior in organizations, I found an author by the name of Russell Ackoff—specifically his book *The Art of Problem Solving*. In it, he talks about ideals, suggesting that these are distal goals that are intrinsic; while they are important in driving behavior, Ackoff argues, what one really needs to be concerned with are *proximal* goals, which are extrinsic (White Board Illustration 7.3). This idea, once understood, helped me understand my own behavior, my father's in hindsight, and continues to help me daily as I lead both my family and my business.

Allow me to elaborate. In my family business world (the one we presumably share), I uphold continuity to be my ideal. In other words, my distal valued outcome is the continuity of our family business. While this is something I strive for, it really is intangible, and though I can visualize it, there are far too many variables in play that can influence this outcome. My efforts thus need to be on *proximal* outcomes, which are tangible things

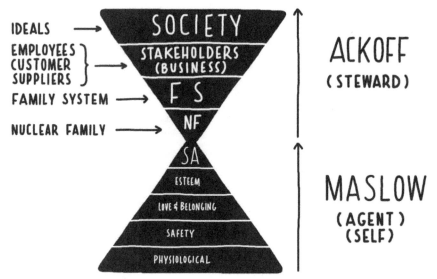

White Board Illustration 7.2. Maslow's Pyramid and Ackoff's Ideals: My Hour Glass Framing

White Board Illustration 7.3. Ideals = Distal and Intrinsic

that I can influence. I include the governance initiatives, the systems and structures I drive, as examples of these proximal goals, which assist me in, hopefully, delivering my distal-valued outcome of continuity. I consider this as fundamental to understanding being a steward.

The O'Reilly Family: Illustrative Story

Consider this example of a steward in action. O'Reilly's Rainforest Retreat, Villas and Lost World Spa, is a family-owned and operated business that was first established in 1926 as a guesthouse in the Lamington National Park in Queensland, Australia. The business has developed an international reputation in ecotourism and is the winner of numerous training, family business, and tourism industry awards. Over the past 90 years, successive generations of O'Reillys have become renowned for their stewardship of the external physical environment as they pioneered the development of ecotourism. In recent decades they have embraced stewardship more fully to define family motivations and their firm's orientation.

The O'Reilly family have invested in the development of professional family governance processes to not only guide their business governance but also articulate, refine, and preserve shared values. These shared values, and the professionalized processes used to regularly confirm these values, enable identification with the firm especially for those later-generation members not working in the business. Central to these values is the respect for the hard work and ethics displayed by O'Reilly ancestors in building the family's reputation for legendary hospitality. The family's enduring mission is to preserve these heritage values through an LTO that suppresses short-term financial return in favor of survival for subsequent generations. The recent global financial crisis (GFC) called on family owners to demonstrate their perseverance to help the firm survive, providing a real case of stewardship in action.

A Focus on Stewardship—Supported by Governance and Values

The current managing director (CEO) of the family business learned business outside the family business in the hospitality industry both in Australia and overseas. The family had been pursuing a professionalization agenda for a number of years; included among the professional measures are both an active board of directors and regular family meetings.

The board of directors meets 8–10 times each year and is chaired by a nonfamily independent director and has over the years included up to two other independent nonfamily directors. The family has also been holding family meetings since the early 1990s, driven by the need to innovate. These family meetings have now evolved to include an annual general meeting of the company in which the chair and CEO account to the family as "owners." These meetings are typically held over two days and include all family members and spouses/partners.

In the context of these meetings some years ago they utilized a process that unearthed the values and expectations of second-, third-, and fourth-generation family members. Under facilitation these were distilled as a shared set of values, which I have listed in Table 7.1.

These values not only guide board deliberations but also are reflective of key heritage values. Second-generation coleader Peter O'Reilly often draws the family's attention to the contributions of the founders,

Table 7.1 Family as Family, Community, Owners, Employees

Family as family	• To encourage all family members (including those not working in the business) to contribute to the perpetuation of the family's values by their representation of the family in various forums
	• To further improve communication, especially to celebrate milestones that will be maintained in part via internal newsletters
	• To encourage family to stay (holiday/visit regularly) in the mountain resort
	• To ensure the development of succession plans and to consider developing more flexibility to enable the identification of exit strategies for those needing them
Family as community	• To be known as a leader of ecotourism in Australia
	• To build further the family's reputation as ethical, honest, fair, and supporters of the broader local community
	• To be known as an employer of choice
	• To recognize the indigenous heritage of the region
Family as owners	• To grow the family business
	• To consolidate the guesthouse operation
	• To diversify and grow the business, thereby providing increased opportunities for family to work and have career paths within the business
	• To implement structures (i.e., ownership, financial, strategic) to aid this growth and diversification

Family as employees	• To encourage family members to pursue career options via employment in the diversified business
	• To develop two distinct employment policies for family members: (1) for operations (lower level/ internships and vacation employment) and (2) for management
	• To emphasize that respect has to be earned and is a vital part of the company framework. A separate induction program will be required for family members so that they know and appreciate the extra demands and expectations placed on them in the family business work environment

Source: Ken Moores and Justin Craig, "From Vision to Variables: a Scorecard to Continue the Professionalization of a Family Firm." In *The Handbook of Research on Family Business*, edited by P. Z. Poutziouris, K. X. Smyrnios, and S. B. Klein. Edward Elgar Publisher, in association with IFERA—The International Family Enterprise Research Academy, 2006, pp. 201–202.

especially their hard work, passion, and commitment. In his recent book *The Spirit of O'Reillys: The World at Our Feet,* he observed:

> My aunts and uncles were the strength behind the original O'Reilly's Guest House. They built it on top of a mountain in the most isolated of places and showed the passion and commitment to run it for thirty years. (p. 130)

When Peter and his elder brother Vince took over leadership of the guesthouse, he noted:

> If Vince and I were going to gain an interest in the business in the future, it would be by acquiring shares in the company. At this early stage running the business was more of a concern to us and we gave very little thought to the eventual ownership of it. (p. 257)

If ever there was an example of being a steward, then this surely is it. But Peter's respect for past generations is also matched by his confidence for the current generation when he recently noted:

> As we know, family businesses are subject to the same disciplines of any business, and family members must be prepared to work hard and get on together. It is pleasing to see this happening in the third generation and the dedication they show to the Guest House is outstanding. I have every confidence in them. (p. 267)

The family feels strongly that the business continues to acknowledge the history of its foundation by perpetuating the values of prior generations and developing flexible ownership structures to enable continued generational involvement. Also, family members are united especially in their goal to emphasize environmental stewardship, an acknowledged central ideology of founding generations.

A Challenging Test

The LTO of the family owners was drawn on heavily over recent years when the effects of the GFC and the subsequent world events that had detrimental impacts on especially Australia's tourism industry affected the family business. They had to dig deep and demonstrate their resilience. Their perseverance was really needed to ensure their survival, and family members demonstrated a real patience concerning capital by foregoing any hope of immediate returns so as to sustain the business for the longer term. This was challenging especially when several banks were forced by the short-term interests of their shareholders to adopt somewhat harsh measures. But with hard work, professionalism, and the perseverance of family owners the O'Reillys have endured these circumstances in the interests of creating opportunities for future generations.

O'Reilly's leaders really capture what it takes to be a steward, as demonstrated by their handling of GFC-related challenges. I urge you to take special note and look to learn from examples like this because you don't really know what it means until you live it, and you most likely will at some point on your watch as a leader.

Summary

Family business leaders must understand what being a steward involves. From what I have observed and experienced, it really is a major foundation of what distinguishes family from nonfamily businesses. The individual dimensions of stewardship (i.e., intrinsic motivation, high identification with the business, and use or personal rather than positional power), when interpreted in tandem with the organizational dimensions (collectivist culture, power distance, involvement) and the related concepts of LTO, ideals and goals, and servant leadership, have become fundamental to better positioning myself for my role as leader of the family and the business.

Trilogy of Lessons for Best Practice Long-Term Stewardship

Lesson 1: Stewards are intrinsically motivated.

Lesson 2: Ownership involves a higher purpose.

Lesson 3: Leaders are also servants.

Exemplar Story: The Steward

The 55-year-old was troubled. He was one of five fourth-generation (G4) members of a family that ran a 125-year-old Asia-based food and health product giant. As chairman of the Family Office, he was deeply concerned about how best to increase involvement of the fifth generation (G5), his children's cohort. Out of the 14 G5 members (all but three between ages 20 and 30), only two had joined the business, and very few others expressed interest in involvement. No G5 cousins were currently taking advantage of the company's internship opportunities, and there was little interest in the family's mentoring program.

"Whatever we're doing isn't working," he said to himself. Others shared his frustration, including his 56-year-old sister who ran the Family Learning and Development Center which offered multiple training and orientation programs, a business strategy workshop, and tuition for family business courses at universities. She observed that the younger-generation members were busy with outside interests, including marriage, emerging careers, and hobbies. Yet the lack of interest in business and governance roles was also part of a growing pattern of low family engagement, such as the cancellation of recent family retreats (once an annual tradition) due to some family conflict and apathy.

A history of clashes and splits among past generations of the family regarding business leadership made the engagement issue even more meaningful and urgent. In the 1970s, the G4 siblings' father and his two brothers (G3 members) had a falling out over direction of the company, and their father bought out his brothers and significantly grew the business. Their father and mother were now in their 80s and still involved in the business. Their five children all joined the business in the 1980s after obtaining college degrees overseas in food science, chemical engineering, marketing, and finance. In the 2000s, they started and grew successfully a new division of health products.

The fifth generation had attended private international, religious, or foreign boarding schools and colleges. From childhood, their experience with the business had been more limited than that of their parents. Their far-flung schooling and time-consuming independent activities also made it difficult for them to develop strong relationships among their cousins. G5's primary sources of information about the company were quarterly e-mail updates from the Family

Office, along with their parents' comments at home and informally during the weekly family dinners they attended when in their home country.

The Family Office chairman was saddened by G5's lack of involvement. He felt that he hadn't accomplished much by way of motivating the next generation—an objective he'd made a primary focus at this stage of his career. "What I worry about is whether we can or can't pass on the passion, the competence, the understanding for involvement in our enterprise. We need ideas that work better."

The chairman felt that the future success of the business likely rested on stimulating the interest of the fifth generation to contribute their ambition and skills to it. Without their efforts, the family's vision of continuing as a role-model family enterprise was unlikely to be realized.

This exemplar story is based on the following case study: John Ward, Carol Adler Zsolnay, and Sachin Waikar, *How to Motivate the Fifth Generation? Balancing Engagement and Entitlement at Lee Kum Kee*, Kellogg Case #5-214-251, published 2016.

Stewart's Takeaways from the Exemplar Story: The Steward

- *Even a company many generations old that has undertaken measures to instill LTO has no guarantee that stewardship behavior to sustain the business will emerge within all generations, at different stages of their individual life cycles.*
- *Questions to ask ourselves as leaders:*
  - *How much should parents encourage/attract the next generation's interest versus let them find their own way?*
  - *How do potential successors come to know enough to have an informed opinion of their possible interest?*
  - *What are effective ways to educate and prepare successors for family business governance?*
  - *How can successors be encouraged to feel the responsibilities of family business ownership as an opportunity rather than a burden?*

CHAPTER EIGHT

The Architect

I attempt to bring the spirit of the founder, my grandmother Ruth, into every decision I make for the company.
—Cindi Bigelow, Third-Generation Leader,
Bigelow Tea Company

In the earlier section related to architecture, I shared how I saw family businesses as designed differently from other types of firms. In this section, I move the level of analysis to the individual designer: *the architect*. The role of the business family architect cannot be understated. *Space, light,* and *form* are the bedrock of being a successful "regular" architect— and I don't see it as much different for a business family architect. In other words, the design needs to allow sufficient space for current- and next-generation members and nonfamily stakeholders to function individually and collectively; it should bring in sufficient light to facilitate growth and allow for diverse opinions to thrive (or as someone reminded me, "Sunshine is an effective disinfectant. Best to air your grievances in the sunshine"), but it needs robust form to withstand, what are at times, significant shocks.

Further, from my unashamedly simplistic view of the world, a lot of what is different about that which distinguishes family businesses is encapsulated in how their architects design structures to manage conflict. Recall from the earlier chapter that introduced architecture as that which dictates both organizational activities and the authority and autonomy of those designated to undertake the activities, which will determine the managerial control systems, and the functional systems in place, including performance, human resources, and marketing.

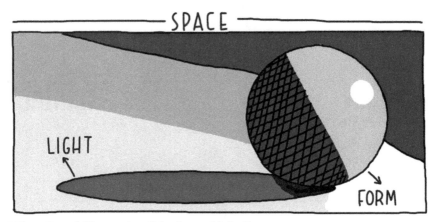

White Board Illustration 8.1. Space Light Form

In this chapter, I will focus on conflict and why I think it is particularly important for the architect. You may get the impression that I have become something of a "conflict junkie," and I admit that is intentional because I have. I will also include the story of someone I see as the definitive architect who has used structures and systems to bring transparency and reduce conflict to his family company, an enterprise which, for me, is aspirational (White Board Illustration 8.1).

Conflict

Conflict, for many, is a forbidden zone. Conflict for the family business leader is very much part of our/your territory. It is one of those inevitabilities I have come to embrace rather than avoid. Actually, the more I have to live with conflict in its many manifestations, the more I have come to appreciate that, in fact, it is not such a bad thing and, if managed, can contribute to better individual and organizational performance. Becoming a better manager of conflict has made me a better leader. Designing structures that facilitate figurative space, light, and form have helped me harness the positives of conflict and reduce its negative consequences. Or put another way, conflict management does not necessarily imply avoidance, reduction, or termination of conflict. Instead, it involves designing effective strategies to minimize the dysfunctions of conflict and strengthening its constructive functions to enhance the effectiveness and longevity of your business and family. As you process my musings in this section, it's critical to understand that so much of conflict comes from conclusions based on faulty assumptions, which, in my mind, highlights the paramount role of the architect in designing forums to ensure assumptions—and expectations—are articulated.

Recall that I am an emergent conflict management junkie, not an expert (on this or anything, it could be argued). However, in my pursuit of better understanding, I note that all the "theorists"—that is, sociologists, economists, political scientists, anthropologists, and psychologists—have a great deal to say about conflict of one sort or another. My understanding is that the early "ists" assumed conflict in organizational settings was detrimental but that in more recent times that view has changed.

Conflict in any organization, fundamentally, results from a breakdown in the standard mechanisms of decision making, which causes individuals or groups to experience difficulty in selecting an alternative or path. I like this definition: "An interactive state in which the behaviors or goals of one actor are to some degree incompatible with the behaviors or goals of some other actor or actors"—it describes what I often observe when trying to make sense of a situation.

There are two origin points of organizational conflict:

1. Within a person
2. Between two or more people

These points form the foundation for three levels of organizational conflict: *intrapersonal, intragroup,* and *intergroup.* Intrapersonal conflict occurs when a member of an organization is required to perform certain tasks, activities, or roles that do not match his or her expertise, interests, goals, or values. Intragroup conflict occurs as a result of disagreements or inconsistencies among the members of a group or between subgroups within a group. Intergroup conflict refers to disagreements or inconsistencies between the members or their representatives or leader of two or more groups. I encourage you to interpret each of these levels in your own idiosyncratic, individual, family, and business contexts.

Conflict in Family Business

Although family business as a field of study is relatively new, organizational conflicts in family business are well documented. They have provided rich backgrounds for novelists, playwrights, filmmakers, and soap opera producers, for example, for longer than we care to remember. The popular press has also long fed on the intrigue surrounding business families in conflict. In family firms, conflict is often seen as promoting self-interest (i.e., self-interested agents) and thus as running against the basic tenets of the family business, including the potential disruption of shared values, vision, and objectives.

Sources of Conflict

Fundamentally, the high amount of conflict in family business—and low number of businesses passed on successfully to the next generation—can be related to the lack of an insightful architect responsible for facilitating structures and processes to address the inherent problem caused by the overlap of the business (capitalist) and family (social) systems. The sources of conflict in the family business created by this overlap, and of which the architect should be mindful, include

- ambiguity of roles and rules in the family business,
- difference in power or status among family and nonfamily members,
- a hasty and/or unfair succession process,
- rivalries among family members (in particular the founder's offspring),
- the favorite son/daughter syndrome,
- lack of clear and coherent policies regarding career development, compensation, and hiring,
- lack of a code of conduct, and
- lack of job descriptions and clear boundaries.

As families and business exist for fundamentally different reasons—the family to care for and nurture its members, the business to profit economically through the production of goods or services—the architect must live in two worlds concurrently. The architect must understand, for example, that the design must facilitate the inclusion of family members in a business setting, which can create a dedicated, motivated workforce more committed to business success than typical employees would be, or, alternatively, result in the business displaying the characteristics of nepotism. In the most negative sense, the situation can result in either (1) unqualified, unmotivated workers, performing poorly, yet feeling protected by their family status, or (2) frustrated, powerless workers unable to overcome the limitations of coworkers who are also family members.

Avoiding conflict is counterproductive, but despite this, the pressure on a family firm to maintain an image of cohesiveness may serve to suppress family conflicts. However, my experience suggests business family conflict may be suppressed for other reasons. I know because, as an architect, I have used these contributing factors to design preventive structures. Specifically:

1. First, the economic interdependence between the family and the business may make it difficult for people to tell one another when their needs for belonging, influence, and intimacy are not being met.
2. Second, although the business may be seen as an intrusive "third party" in the family's life, for those involved to "bite the hand that feeds you" may be viewed as problematic.
3. Third, in many traditional family-owned businesses, family members view the father/founder as a powerful or larger-than-life figure.

In a study that really resonates with me, the focus was on conflict that arises between fathers and sons around issues of control, power, and competition. The authors found that such conflict makes communication between fathers and sons difficult. This conflict is often connected with the father's desire that the business do well, that his hard-won achievements not be undermined, and that his expertise be put to good use, and with the son's conflicting desires for autonomy and parental control. I went through this with my dad to some extent and am preparing to go through it again with my son, but obviously from a different vantage.

When the architect does not design for the transfer of ownership and power, the level of individuation and maturation possible for family members is limited. In our family business world, even the simplest principle of "every child gets treated fairly" is tested routinely. Equal treatment becomes a problem due to different talents, interests, activities, and circumstances. Thus, many family conflicts in business stem from balancing family notions of fairness.

In general, sons working in family firms have a long history of conflict with their fathers. Such conflict is expected as the son forms his own identity and seeks his own power. This topic could take up an entire chapter if not another whole book. Several authors have proposed that competition between a father and a son can be seen as resulting from the son's desire to be like the father, to emulate him, to "become the father." If you are really interested, I think Shakespeare had a thing or two to say on this topic, as did the Greek dramatists before him.

I enjoy picking up "tips" from others, particularly when I observe a "solution in action." Sometimes these nuggets don't come from the source but from others who are somehow connected to the family in business conversation. A great example of this was when a friend shared a story of someone he knew who was able to orchestrate his offspring being able to get along from an early age. When asked why his children got along as well as they did, he explained that they learned to negotiate through their shared interest in water skiing. He explained that the sport required a minimum of three to be involved: one to drive the boat, one to observe, and obviously one to ski. Therefore, if anyone of them wanted to ski, he or she had to negotiate with two others, a practical solution with lasting benefit.

To summarize, avoidance of conflict in family business can be a real problem. In trying to avoid destructive conflict, the constructive conflict that is necessary for a company to grow is also avoided. Many families attempt to avoid conflict, wrongly believing the common myth that conflict is bad and wrong if people love each other. In truth, individuals do not always agree with people they love, and, in fact, individuals do not usually have conflicts with people they don't care about. Every family business conflict has an emotional component that must be addressed along with the practical issue at stake. The architect's role is to introduce appropriate structures to circumvent the inevitability that conflict will occur and need to be managed.

Willow Ware Australia: Illustrative Story

In order to better comprehend the important role of the architect in designing and driving the implementation of appropriate structures, consider the case of the iconic Wilson family from Australia. The current family leader is a great example of an architect who is able to reduce tension across the business and the family systems by focusing on architecture. It is truly a great story and one that I count among the best I have seen—and that says a lot.

The story starts way back on July 29, 1887, when Ralph and Richard Wilson began building metal working machinery and tools. They worked in a shed at the rear of their family home in Flemington, Victoria, using a lathe, straight edge, cold chisel, hammer, and file. Pioneer manufacturers in those days waged a war of savage competition not for the faint of heart. Among men of limited capital, only those with an immense appetite for work and a capacity for frugal living made the grade. They were in survival mode every day.

The original Ralph (each leader to the present day is named Ralph) was a man of exceptional inventive gifts combined with practical ingenuity. Applying himself to the technical problems of fabrication using tin, he designed and built by hand an extraordinary range of presses and machines, some of which are still in use today. In 1930 Ralph, the founder, died. Willow came under the leadership of his only son, Ralph, who had worked to rebuild and improve the procedures of the tiring business during the 1920s. Following this, the business went on to survive the Great Depression, World War II, raw material shortages, and further financial hardships. Despite all of this, the business was successfully transferred from one generation to the next, and Ralph V, my mate, son of the present proprietor, joined the firm in 1978.

To survive and thrive when many other manufacturers did not, the company kept no "sacred cows" in its divisions or properties. Only its ethic and determination to survive and succeed were inviolable (read, collective culture a stewardship dimension). In conjunction with becoming a more modern and efficient manufacturing organization, the company further professionalized by strengthening its marketing and sales areas to assist in the provision of improved strategic direction. Product ranges have been rationalized or extended where relevant, allowing core competencies in business units to be developed to market leadership.

Willow has successfully transitioned the business from one generation to the next despite the considerable hardships faced by the business to date. Ralph Wilson (the current fifth-generation family CEO) attributes this to constant professionalization of the family business. He, like his forebears, is a true architect. He credits designing the financial and operational control systems in order to ensure the decentralization of authority (operational) and top-level activeness as key to the professionalization of his family's firm. More specifically:

1. Financial (and operational) control systems

   Our financial control systems and procedures really assist in the strategic decision making and help us to achieve shareholder expectations.

Throughout the long history and evolution of Willow Ware Australia, key decisions have been made on the back of good data. It prides itself on the quality of its financial and operational control systems. These systems and processes enable the business management to make crucial (often hard) decisions regarding the continuation and introduction of product lines.

2. Decentralization of authority

   It has been a useful and positive part of the Willow professionalization process—another strategic initiative that assists us in achieving stakeholder expectations.

Human resource systems and structures contribute to a culture and philosophy that enables the senior executive team to focus their efforts on strategic direction—working on the business rather than in the business—but still being active within business management. Providing individuals with the authority to make decisions is empowering, providing this is measured by responsibility and accountability.

3. Top-level activeness

    This has also been a vital contributor to the professionalization process. Throughout the five generations of Wilson ownership of Willow Ware Australia, the family have been active participants at the management and governance levels. Their strategic input and independence of thought have helped the organization to survive tough economic times, make difficult decisions regarding product lines, and steward the business for future generations.

The Wilson family have survived many family and business challenges since their founding in 1887. Pivotal to their ability to continue, they claim, is the architecture that has been introduced by a procession of leaders and which delivers conflict-reducing accountability and timely and effective decision making.

Summary

I am constantly aware of the need to design architecture to reduce the negative effects of conflict and build trust within the various family and business teams that make up our increasingly complex ecosystem. I am reminded daily of the existence of conflict across my family and business, and am not naïve to think that this will always sort itself out. At the end of the day, you see, it really is about space, light, and form.

Trilogy of Lessons for Best Practice Long-Term Stewardship

Lesson 1: The architect is the designer of family and business trust mechanisms, which reduce negative conflict.

Lesson 2: Informed ownership requires an understanding of the architect's design plans.

Lesson 3: Good architectural design is fruitless without implementation.

Exemplar Story: The Architect

En route to visit his family's historic, palatial ancestral home in a small village in southern India, the 61-year-old, G3 family chairman of the Family's Corporate

Board (FCB) pondered the best organizational strategy for his Family Group (FG) and his role within it.

FG was a long-standing Indian family enterprise established in the 1910s. By the mid-2000s the firm was India's 16th-largest business group, with revenues of $850 million and over 23,000 employees delivering products and services ranging from abrasives to door frames to mutual funds. Until 1990, its seven companies were each headed by a family-member CEO, with no formal interaction among the businesses as a group and limited, informal consultations among family members.

In 1990, FG family members chose to formalize group management by creating the FCB. This move was primarily in response to India's fast-changing business environment: the economy was increasingly liberalized, generating significant new opportunities (e.g., more exporting) and threats (e.g., greater domestic and foreign competition) that required speedier, more flexible, and less emotionally driven business portfolio decisions than the group had made before. In 1999 family members took the unprecedented step of separating ownership and operational management of the seven companies, promoting nonfamily managers to CEO roles. The five family members who had headed the companies moved into shared office quarters to become full-time directors of the reorganized FCB, joined by three independent outside board members and the group's nonfamily CFO.

Now, in the mid-2000s, the group is continuing to adjust to the modified governance structure and India's ongoing economic shifts. In this context the family chairman of the FCB considered the company's future. He believed that further professionalization was necessary to ensure the group's ongoing success but recognized that the business was still adjusting to the recent reorganization and market changes. He also knew that if he followed the cultural precedent of his brother and uncle, he had only four years until mandatory retirement at age 65.

In addition, the family chairman faced the possibility of taking on another traditional role in his family. He knew that eventually, when his older brother died, he would be the oldest male family member and called upon to serve as the family's "Kartha," the elder expected to direct the academic and professional paths of other members and oversee major business decisions. He did not feel that he had the temperament nor abilities needed to do that expected role well with the 30+ family members. In advance of that role being bestowed on him, he worked to alter the precedent of the eldest male being head both of the family and of the business. He split the roles going forward, so the best male family member, not just the eldest, would be assigned to each role.

This exemplar story is based on the following case study: John Ward and Carol Adler Zsolnay, *The Murugappa Group: Centuries-Old Business Heritage and Tradition*, Kellogg Case #5-104-011, published 2004.

Stewart's Takeaways from the Exemplar Story: The Architect

- *As a leader with his architect's hat on, it is important to contemplate not only one's own roles but also how the family business needs to be reshaped in an ever-changing environment.*

- *Cultural norms and family traditions may conflict with the best interests of the enterprise—and those might also be the best interests of the family, in this case, the need to professionalize, to structure the business differently, and to put in place the best person to lead the family, even if that is not the eldest male, who fills that role traditionally.*

- *As leaders we should each look what cultural, economic, and political expectations have shaped strategy, issues, and structures of our family business, and not be afraid to explore options of change that are contrary to what has occurred in the past.*

CHAPTER NINE

The Governor

What you have inherited from your father, you must earn over again for yourselves, or it will not be yours.
—Johann Wolfgang von Goethe

In the previous individual-focused chapters related to the leader's role as steward and architect, I made a concerted effort to make the concepts less "technical" and thus relatively easy to grasp, at the risk of oversimplifying. Here, my intent is to share with you some important (quasi) technical skills that I have learned in my role as a governor. In fact, I should say in my *roles* as governor because I have had to develop a distinct mind-set and refine my skillset for each governing role I've undertaken within our family. The obvious governing role is as a director of our family business. Over recent years this has been complemented by my roles governing the *family* itself and helping to steward our wealth as my governance journey leads us to move toward introducing a family office. Therefore, my focus in this chapter will be the mind-set needed to be a governor in whatever capacity and the associated skills required to effectively discharge those responsibilities (White Board Illustration 9.1).

These mind-sets and skillsets are on display when family governors *enter* and *engage* with the family and business. Of equal importance, however, there is need for governor-like qualities when leaders are planning to *exit* the business, as well. Governors approaching exit set a departure date and announce it publicly, thus committing themselves to the goal of transferring power within an established time frame. Making the date public lends a sense of urgency to planning for the inevitable transition and helps to enlist other key management personnel, employees, suppliers, and customers in the process. In our case, the discipline provided by having a fixed time frame enabled family members, both within and outside the business, to work busily and determinedly to accomplish a smooth succession, one that has contributed deeply to our enterprise's sustainability and continuity.

To define governance, the needs and characteristics of the entity being governed—whether the family, family business, or family office—need to be acknowledged. Moreover, while governance does not necessarily require three separate governing bodies, having more than one will likely prove beneficial. Of these I have found my family governor role most critical, since the goals to be achieved within the family entity are to be served by both the family business and, eventually, the family office. In short, being a family governor helped me to better frame my additional governing duties in other family entities. Accordingly, I will start with lessons learned about being an effective family governor before sharing my thoughts on governing our business.

Family Governor

To be an effective family governor typically entails leadership at the family level—leadership that helps stewards, architects, and entrepreneurs to function. While some governors also act out all or some of these other roles, I have observed that they generally adopt a mind-set focused strongly on remaining as a family-in-business. They see both family and business benefits from continuing in this manner, and they champion the cause of developing the family-ownership advantage by investing energy into the family-business system. Therefore, it's not surprising that such leaders often emerge as chairs of family councils.

In this capacity, the leaders' mind-set is one focused on developing family owners into a more engaged, active, stronger group. Unlike leaders or governors of business, they are often not appointed but instead emerge as family leaders based on their display of vision, energy, and inspiration. They strive to develop the family as responsible owners and stewards of the business by working in conjunction with business governors (directors) to ensure mutually aligned and beneficial coordination between business and family. In this way family governors contribute to the success of the business by promoting aligned governance structures of a family council and board of directors. The critical characteristic shared by the most effective family governors is that their mind-set is flexible in promoting an overall process that creates an integrated system of governance across all family entities; that is, family governors work as key players in the system by engaging as many family members as possible in a cycle of engagement among individual, family, and business that is ongoing, dynamic, and never really "completed."

The skillset of family governors who champion integrated governance processes in this way includes strong interpersonal competencies. This requires listening well, communicating effectively, and integrating complementary perspectives from within the family group. What I have observed in our family and those of close colleagues is that by acting in this way, successful family governors build credibility and trust by being accountable, transparent, and authentic. In addition to these interpersonal and communication skills, family governors typically have a keen interest in learning and engage in ongoing educational opportunities to complement their diverse personal and professional experience.

By inspiring and encouraging family to become owners dedicated to a common goal, these governors help create a *community* dedicated to being responsible stewards and building a family legacy. This helps the family to develop its collective communication abilities, which in turn enables better management of intergenerational dynamics. From my observations, these family leaders help to develop the family to be a truly advantageous resource for the enterprise.

Not surprisingly family governors champion both education and communication within the family and between the family and its affiliated entities. To achieve this, they have a mind to ensure that they and all others respect the past while accepting their collective responsibilities to steward the family's business and wealth to better places for subsequent generations. In this sense, good family governors reflect a strong learning orientation and encourage others within the family to be likeminded.

To refine their own broad range of skills while developing them among the wider family, family governors favor education based on discussion and consideration of family history and virtues, duties of responsible owners, roles family members can and do play, and the surfacing and clarification of any unspoken rules within the family. Moreover, family governors draw upon "social secretary" skills and event-planning capabilities to provide venues and opportunities for expression of ideas and opinions, along with events to foster family unity and sense of connection. In these ways, they help to steward the next generation's dreams.

Business Governor

These lessons have not only added to my skillset but also influenced my mind-set when discharging my responsibilities as a governor in the family business. The first key aspect that I have learned about business governance, or being a governor/director, is that to be effective you need discipline—that is, discipline to understand that your responsibility is to the *business*, not to the constituency that placed you in the governor role. Thus, your mind-set must be to represent all and not simply a select few. I stress that now and likely a few more times in this section.

In order to discharge your duty as a governor of your business, you will need to remember that you have to think and behave differently than you do in your other roles (steward, architect, and entrepreneur). I think of it as the governor role effectively usurping the other roles; that is, as a business governor I not only have responsibility to the business, management, family, and broader community but also have obligations dictated by law. The exact legal circumstances vary by jurisdiction, but I am convinced that how you behave as a governor should be the same, regardless.

The Three Ps

Family-owned firms have governance advantages in terms of their propensities for value creation. The unification of ownership and control literally consolidates organizational authority into the hands of the entrepreneur. Therefore, to get a handle on the mind-set needed to be an effective family business governor in this context, I went in search of some descriptive features.

In my readings, I came across a set of features that appeared to align with my observations of the world of family business governance. Yes, the frame was built around three central ideas—three Ps in fact: *parsimony, personalism,* and *particularism.* These terms might be a bit off-putting at first, but on further examination they are relatively simple. In fact, they not only describe the behavioral traits of family business governors but, in so doing, also effectively outline the mind-set adopted by these governors: a mind-set through which family business governors differ from those directing and controlling other entities.

Parsimony simply means being frugal. People are more prudent with their own money, and family business governors have strong incentives to ensure capital is deployed sparingly and used intensively. In short, they carefully conserve resources when governing.

Personalism means that family owners can project their own vision into the business and the governor is subject to far fewer internal and external constraints. These fewer constraints enable governors to see the firm as their own, and to employ particularistic criteria of their own choosing when making decisions.

This *particularism* will not always be expressed in rational-calculative criteria based on value maximization, but will on occasion be reflective of more subjective concerns of the family owners. (Carney 2005)

Effective Governance

To govern competently, I maintain, requires a genuine understanding of what it is you are governing and for whom. This sounds basic, but trust me, in the family-owned business context it can be far from simple. Therefore, let me throw out some ideas about what it is you are responsible for governing. Simple answer: the business. But the family business, as I have alluded to throughout this book, has characteristics that are not as evident in nonfamily businesses. My approach, then, is to understand I am concurrently responsible for governing two critical things: my forebears' legacy and my offspring's destiny. And to do so effectively requires me to forecast both the economic and social outcomes of my decisions. In this way, my governor role complements my steward role in which I adopt a long-term perspective when making decisions for those who have entrusted me to govern on their behalf.

To make decisions as a governor, I have learned that the role calls for a different modus operandi than that of being a manager of the business. The mind-set and skills required are different. Apart from the aforementioned need to decide what's best for all, I often have to make decisions with less than perfect information—sometimes far less. In short, as a governor I must make judgments. This requires certain thinking skills that the boffins refer to as "cognitive skills." My way of doing this is to approach every decision from two angles. I first craft my *thesis*; I then spin this around deliberately to create an *antithesis*, and with these both in play I *synthesize* the two alternate viewpoints. This takes discipline and mastering, what someone described as "artful procrastination." To some observers it may seem that I am not efficient and even uncertain, but in reality I am seeking solutions that may not always be immediately evident. My purpose, as suggested earlier, is to discharge my duty as a director to the business within the context of past and future generations. In short, I never make a decision before I have to, despite the fact that many seem to associate real leadership with rapid decision making. The trick lies in being artful without excessive procrastination.

As noted, a crucial aspect of this process that I (thankfully) have mastered is the understanding that I will never get perfect information. Thus, I need to access the best information I can and not stall the entrepreneurial process on which our business relies. My role as a director is not to inhibit this spirit but to *activate* it, as it is my belief that this is where our distinctive capabilities as business families lie. Therefore, my message to you is to develop a tolerance of ambiguity. I certainly have.

Another distinguishing feature of my role as a governor is that this decision making is and should be collegial: To be successful as a governor, a key skill I have mastered is the need to *persuade* and be *persuadable*. When I first heard of this requirement for an optimally contributing governor, I was taken by the simplicity of the message, and I am all about simple messaging! To persuade requires a fine-tuned capacity to provide a compelling argument aligned closely with the agreed-upon strategy and embedded firmly in the values and beliefs of the family. This brings into play the importance of strategic planning and a genuine understanding of family values. Without these, how, pray tell, can anyone provide direction? But equally I have learned that there is no point in attending a board meeting with a closed mind. Remember, we are making judgments with less-than-perfect information, and to that end it is best to be open-minded to the prospect that you might be persuaded to support a position quite different from the one you entered with.

Importantly, governor characteristics are on display when *entering* the family business, during *engagement,* and, of course, when *exiting* the business. In addition, leaders are involved in governing their families and perhaps entities that steward their wealth through generations, whether it be a family office or some other structure.

The Dennis Family: Illustrative Story

As with the Market Basket and Willow stories in previous chapters, I will again use a story of a governance-savvy family I know to illustrate and amplify the concepts I've presented. In this instance, the Dennis family are founders of a large real estate and construction company; the founding couple had groomed their four offspring, two sons and two daughters, from early on to be competent business individuals. By adulthood, the children were certainly ready, willing, and very capable. Though confident that the four would be successful separately, if that is what they decided to do, the founders also felt that it would be great if they could combine their strengths and build a sustainable family business for the current and future generations. They did not want to pressure their children into joining forces, and they wanted to make sure that whatever happened was fair to all parties.

A Critical Decision

In general, then, the family were well aware of the challenges that face family businesses when control, management, and ownership issues overlap. With that in mind, they actually asked the "kids" whether they would prefer the parents to work toward a structure that would eventually see the assets that had been built over the initial 25 years liquidated, with the funds divided equally among the children, or whether the four of them would prefer to consolidate the associated businesses with the parent company and take on the challenge of professionalizing this new entity. The sibling-ship expressed unanimous desire to amalgamate and "make a real go of it." The result of the decision to integrate their various interests (in farming, land, development, and consulting) culminated in the first *official* family meeting.

This meeting was a key turning point for the family at which it was established that, at the very least, the various ad hoc arrangements between and among members of the family and generations needed to be formalized. In other words, they needed architecture and governance, by definition, *architects* and *governors*.

Actions decided upon at the meeting follow:

- Establishing a single entity through which the parents and each of the four children (and their families) could retain equal ownership of the family business
- Ensuring that the single entity could withstand individual demands from any of the four children, or their spouses, or future generations

Guiding Values

With all members of the family agreeing to continue the family business for the benefit of current and future generations, they formulated the values and behavioral guidelines they felt would support the family and business best. They are as follows:

- Engender mutual trust, respect, and understanding.
- Deal honestly and openly with each other at all times.
- Maintain and enhance family relationships while recognizing the individual.
- Promote a harmonious and cooperative relationship between family members.

- Provide encouragement and support to each family member.
- Act always in the best interests of the family and the company.

Mission Statement and Early Governance

The first task of the siblings was to draft a mission statement. They decided on:

to build a long-term, sustainable and profitable family business for present and future generations.

The siblings then proceeded to introduce governance to increase transparency and reduce potential for conflict. The governance was based specifically on these concepts:

1. Equality of ownership
2. Development of a sustainable structure
3. Holding of assets in perpetuity for current and future generations
4. Creation of provision for a family member to sell or withdraw from the structure
5. Provision for the incidence of divorce, mental illness, or a family member or spouse "going off the rails"
6. Sharing of dividends equally

Governance Initiatives

By benchmarking themselves against other successful family businesses, over the next five years the family introduced a "copy book" example of governance to their second-generation family business. Initiatives included the following:

1. Appointing external board members following a skill-gap analysis at board level.
2. Overlaying a matrix of board subcommittees (audit, finance, brand/public relations, and marketing), work groups, and project-control groups (PCGs) across the organization. Each of these committees would have a membership of at least two family members (and in some instances such as the finance subcommittee, an external director), the CEO, and relevant senior executives as required. This structure enables family members to be aware of what is going on with the business while permitting the business to proceed without family members as bottlenecks.

3. Giving the (nonfamily) CEO complete day-to-day responsibility and autonomy.

4. Ensuring the organization is governed by a detailed set of policies and procedures that enable it to function without continual reference to the family members.

5. Adopting a formal dividends policy, equity limits, and financial measures such as a specified weighted average cost of capital.

6. Ensuring that the board does not deal with family issues, which are left to the Family Council.

7. Engaging external consultants to help determine remuneration for family members employed by or consulting to the business.

8. Introducing an annual performance appraisal of all directors.

9. Setting all directors' remuneration to market rates.

10. Structuring the business so that the shareholders (family members) do not run the business; the CEO and senior executive team do, in accordance with the board's strategy and three-year plan.

In Their Words

The central family governor, the second eldest of the siblings, shared his experience of the challenges involved in the transition to professionalization and in driving the process of conceiving and introducing the new structures and systems:

> Initially I wouldn't have thought it was as going to be as challenging, or as comprehensive but by the same token I probably did not envision that it would be as satisfying when it was all finally in place. You do reach a point where you can sit back and look over the business and feel "we have done it." We feel what we have been able to do is very sustainable because everything we have done now is all so defined that if an issue arises there is an appropriate forum in which to deal with it and there is not the gray area in deciding whether something is a family or a business issue. Having said that, we still have circumstances where issues arise because they are not particular to the forum which we are in, but everybody has been through the process now and none of us really have a problem with one saying to the other, "Look, this is not a board issue, let us take it up with the Family Council." Or in the Family Council, "This is an operational issue." Nobody is suppressed with what they want to say. I think it took everybody a long time to understand and respect the structure and it is easy to slip back into old ways. You've got to continually work at it, making sure that the forum that you are in is the appropriate forum to discuss things.

The governor further explained how the family agreed on the often complex, often conflict-causing issue of remuneration:

A lot of detail has gone into putting this structure in place. Now, salaries are entirely separate from director's fee, which is entirely separate from dividends. The dividend is determined by the Family Council and is equally distributed, so the gross amount of dividend is determined and that's determined through the Family Council conveying their desire to the board. The board then communicates that to the senior executives and then a combination of the three which is basically the family, the board, and the senior executives saying, "As investors, we know what you want out of the business, but commercially this is what we can afford otherwise you are going to prejudice the performance of the business." So it will be an agreement between the board and the Family Council on what the gross level of the dividend is and when it flows through to the beneficiaries, it flows through in equal proportions, and it is fixed so that one family member cannot increase their shareholding over another family member or assume control. So, the dividend is struck each year and we receive the dividend for being a shareholder in the family business. A commercial rate of director's fee is paid for being a board member and attending on average, a couple of days a month on board duty which is a day's preparation, a day's board meeting plus the occasional board function as required through the month. The third is remuneration according to the employment position within the business. In my case, for instance, I had a formal role and responsibility job description set out and then I went to an external consultancy firm, and said to them, "This is my role, and responsibility description, this is the size of the organization and this is our turnover, number of employees, etc.; benchmark it against similar companies, similar industries, similar positions in other industries and come back with a salary package range." They did that and that was then put to the board. The board, including our external consultants on the board at the time made the decision on what the salary package would be so that my package is totally independent and determined commercially. So, the salary package was not biased, was not based on me as a person or being a family member. It was based on the position, that if I was not taking that position, what would they expect to pay someone else with the necessary skills, knowledge and expertise to fill that position. In addition, the family members that are not actively employed in the family business are remunerated as a consultant to the family business depending on what task they are performing or on the basis of per meeting attendance. So, one of the family members who has her own family business with her husband still attends business meetings, some of the sub-committees and project groups that we have set up, and for attending each meeting she receives a fee. So, there is a very clear definition around what you are paid for, what your responsibilities are, how you are remunerated rather than saying you are paid $X per year and for that you are expected to do a variety of different tasks. There is now clarity and transparency.

Commenting on the role of the board, the governor shared with me:

I think the days of choosing people with general skills rather than industry-specific skills are limited. We want our board members to actively contribute to the business from day one. We want them to spend the majority of their time looking forward strategically. What we have recognized is that if we are to gain the maximum benefit out of external people at board level, we cannot occupy their time sitting around the table arguing about Family Council issues or family employment in the family business. All those issues are removed. Our board meetings are very structured, very formal and because the overall structure that we put in place with the sub-committees and marketing, finance etc. through the organization, all the operational information feeds up through the sub-committees to the board level. So the board is sitting there, looking at very refined, very detailed, very comprehensive board papers which are about ¾ inches thick but structured so that, in the executive summary, you can gain as much or as little about the operating business as you want to. And then, you can scroll down to whatever level you want to because the supporting papers are there and none of it has to do with family issues.

4Rs MATRIX

ROLES	REQUIREMENT	RESPONSIBILITY	REMUNERATION
SHAREHOLDERS	FAMILY MEMBER	• DIVIDEND POLICY • STRATEGIC INVESTMENT POLICY • APPOINT DIRECTORS	DIVIDEND
BOARD MEMBER	SKILLS/EXPERTISE KNOWLEDGE	FIDUCIARY	MARKET SET BOARD FEES
EXECUTIVE/EMPLOYEE	QUALIFICATIONS	POSITION DESCRIPTION	MARKET SET SALARY

White Board Illustration 9.1. The 4Rs Matrix

How the Governance Works

Throughout this process, the governor emerged as the leader of the family business and was also responsible, increasingly, for leading business change. The core essence of the organization's "Welcome to our Family," for example, was articulated with the input of employees. The values that the family has articulated to reinforce this essence in the business are honesty and integrity, quality, passion, caring, and vision. The company vision, based on those values, is: "To develop a market-driven customer-focused organization that generates through its people a profitable and sustainable long-term business."

Senior management was given responsibility for delivering the strategy for zero to three years, with performance measured against budget. Shareholders monitor strategy through formal monthly board meetings, with presentations from the CEO on performance against budget; this may be in relation to a division, business unit, or geographic location. Monthly board meetings also discuss projected performance for the forthcoming month against budget, as well as year to date. Quarterly re-forecasts for end-of-year financials are also provided.

The operating business introduced a range of board subcommittees that meet regularly, with meetings attended by at least two family members as representatives of the board, ensuring continuity and consistency with strategy. Further to the board subcommittees, PCGs (in effect mini-boards) have been established to guide the direction of specific projects or developments. Two family members are also present on each PCG. Family members are not responsible for the delivery of objectives of the board subcommittees and PCGs but participate in order to ensure strategy is followed and the family's knowledge and expertise is passed on. Finally, work groups also operate for specific requirements—including IT, policy and procedures, strategic planning—again with two family members on each. In addition, bimonthly staff communication meetings assemble all staff, enabling them to keep abreast of the company's performance and promoting the flow of information across the organization.

The system of reporting used at the family business is designed deliberately to reduce conflict and increase transparency. The lines of reporting are both vertical and horizontal: vertically through the work groups, PCGs, subcommittees, and board; horizontally within the discipline or function, such as land development, home-building, or marketing.

Governance, Culture, and Community

Linking back to the stewardship dimensions introduced earlier, employees feel that they are part of a corporation that benefits the community through various socially responsible activities; that is, the values of the family are expressed in tangible ways, not just on paper in company documents. Thus, working for the family becomes more than "just a job." Moreover, because strong communication channels have been established throughout the organization, employees are able to contribute to the family's policy of continuing to be good corporate citizens. The family's openness, transparency, and profit-sharing initiatives have ensured that employees at all levels are committed to carrying out the family's stated core values.

A senior manager shared with me his experience of being involved in some of the projects that typify the family's commitment to the communities in which they operate:

> In the country regions we have been focused on assisting disadvantaged families and young people by building homes and donating the profits to the more needy. This has had a dramatic effect on our staff, trades and other community members. Our staff feels a great sense of goodness and self-fulfillment by giving to the less fortunate. Many of our staff and tradespeople have given countless hours to these projects; this, along with the assistance of our company's ability to make it happen, has developed a sense of pride of working for an organization that cares for other people. Companies such as ours can assist others by using our expertise and time, not necessarily simply donating money. As well, in my experience I have found that huge opportunities develop through networking with other people in caring organizations.

The family knows that a crucial part of professionalization is attracting quality employees. Since he formed the company, the founder has always been committed to his employees. Now owners of a family company of considerable size, the family appreciates that as the organization grows, developing a motivated and committed workforce becomes more challenging. Part of the challenge in changing the architecture of the organization was to ensure that the employees were made aware of the benefits of the changes. During the process of professionalization, they have introduced a variety of initiatives that have ensured that the company continues to be a market leader and can therefore attract quality employees. The family actively demonstrates appreciation for employee contributions through policies and activities, including the following:

- Fifty percent of above-budget profit is distributed to staff.
- The family openly states that its priorities are safety, people, product, and profits (which interpreted means that if they get the first three right, the fourth point will happen).
- Commitment to continuous learning for all employees.
- "Open book" policy of accounting and financial reporting.
- Considerable emphasis paid to employee-associated charity initiatives.

An Unexpected Challenge

The lead governor also shared an unexpected challenge the family faces. Specifically, now that the family is so enmeshed in the business, members must maintain ongoing focus on the *family*. He explained:

> One thing that I have noticed recently is that family members need to appreciate their role as *family* members and not be always focused on being *family business* members. For example, when we get together socially, it is important that we are conscious not to fall back to discussing work-related topics continually. There is a forum now for that. For example, dad has a role to play as a grandfather and he needs to appreciate the importance of that role just like I have a role as a dad, a husband and a brother. It is great that we have worked this hard on the business and we are starting to see the results, but we cannot forget that our role as family members is ultimately more important. What I am saying I guess, is that we have to continue to work *on the family* as well as *on the business*.

Related to his role as leading the governance process, he gave one final piece of advice:

> I think that in the early days all of us would have underestimated the time and effort involved in going through the professionalization process and doing it properly. If I was to give advice, that's exactly what it would be: "Don't underestimate how challenging it will be, and at times how difficult it will be, but the benefit that we are getting now is immeasurable."

The Dennis family case highlights the role of the governor in introducing systems and structures (as depicted in White Board Illustration 9.2) to reduce conflict and increase accountability. It also is a good example for

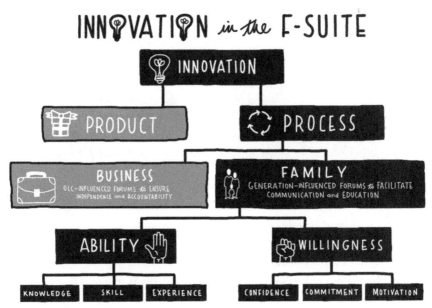

White Board Illustration 9.2. Innovation in the F-Suite, Driving a Governor's Mind-Set

me of the role that governance plays in reducing agency costs and the benefits of stewardship. It should be evident by now how these concepts are all linked and integrated.

Summary

The governor's premise is to promote the understanding that consensus-focused decision making at all levels and in all forums is essential to the long-term success of the family and the business. A healthy appreciation of how a paradoxical approach can actually work is required, specifically that the legacy of the family is the ability to be adaptive and proactive not only in creating wealth but also in creating opportunities for future generations

Trilogy of Lessons for Best Practice Long-Term Stewardship

Lesson 1: Family governors require very particular skillsets.

Lesson 2: Governance systems and structures have far-reaching implications.

Lesson 3: Accountability is an outcome of good governance.

Exemplar Story: The Governor

The nonfamily division vice president and general manager of a large multi-generation family-owned chemical materials enterprise prepared to present a potential plant acquisition to the Environment, Health, and Safety Committee of the board (composed of family and nonfamily independent members). Earlier, he had convinced the division leadership of the strategic value of the purchase and also the urgency of the deal based on the movement of the acquisition's parent company into Chapter 11 bankruptcy and announcement that it would close the plant.

Winning the board's approval was a major challenge for several reasons:

- *It was unclear whether the plant would remain operational.*
- *To run the plant would require the division to enter a shared-services arrangement with the parent company, which continued to use the site.*
- *Making the acquisition would mean integrating its specialized, unionized labor force into the enterprise, which had very few union workers.*
- *Early due diligence had revealed tens of millions of dollars of potential environmental risk on the site.*

The last issue was particularly critical, given the enterprise's generations-long history of respect for the environment and its executives' and board directors' reluctance to take on any business with excessive environmental risk.

Ultimately, the board approved the purchase. The reasons could be construed as counterintuitive. If the enterprise's family business values featured strong environmental protection and sustainability, didn't that suggest that the board would turn down the purchase? Instead, after several iterations of due diligence, risk modeling, and mitigation plans by the division team at the request of directors, the board was persuaded that the values of honoring the natural world, orientation to long-term time horizons, and strategic value to the firm perfectly positioned their enterprise to approve such an outwardly risky purchase. The many issues of the purchase kept competitors from considering it and gave the enterprise a lasting competitive edge. At the end of the longer time horizon, the invested-in acquisition was profitable, growing, and environmentally clean, with the same experienced workforce able to hold on to their jobs.

This exemplar story is based on the following case study: John Ward, Carol Adler Zsolnay, and Sachin Waikar, *A Diamond in the Rough: J. M. Huber and the PATH Business*, Kellogg Case #5-416-757, published 2017.

Stewart's Takeaways from the Exemplar Story: The Governor

- *The executive team and board of a family business (i.e., the governors) work together to evaluate and execute unconventional strategies and tactics, using as guides the family and business values, including respect for all points of view and the willingness to be persuadable.*

- *Marshalling strengths that family enterprises bring to business can be a competitive advantage versus nonfamily firms.*

- *Family business paradoxes can be managed to good result. The division general manager believed in the deal, but it seemed to go against the enterprise's value of environmental sustainability, yet another case where it's not "either/or," but "both/and."*

CHAPTER TEN

The Entrepreneur

Our company does not rest on its 100-year-old heritage. We have a simple product—it's stuff with wheels—but we're very innovative in our space.

—Robert Pasin, Third-Generation Leader, Radio Flyer

I have a confession to make: I approach this chapter with some trepidation. As I noted in the earlier chapter that introduced entrepreneurship, I find conversation around this whole topic to be "loaded." While it's true that I am an entrepreneur on paper, the label does not sit well with me, and I think that's the case for many family business leaders as well, including for the old man (my father and predecessor). We may sometimes struggle to reconcile what we do with the efforts of the young people who start skyrocketing tech businesses or those typically considered "entrepreneurs" by much of society.

Still, if I consider the accepted dimensions of entrepreneurship in the business setting—that is, risk-taking, innovativeness, and proactiveness—I certainly can identify with each of these. But I ask whether this isn't the case for *anyone* involved in commerce, to some degree. Therefore, in this section I will again deliver from a mind-set and skillset perspective how, in my experience, family business leaders are, in fact, entrepreneurs, whether we like this appellation or not. To this end I will focus on the essence of a family business entrepreneur's mind-set before outlining the specific skills needed to behave in this way.

Family Business Leaders *Are* Entrepreneurs

Conventional wisdom would have us believe that we family business leaders are too conservative, excessively frugal with resources, overly emotionally focused, and less economically minded—all mind-sets that get in the way of our ability to innovate and renew businesses. However, I soon discovered that this "wisdom" does not accord with the facts and that as a class we family business leaders adopt different mind-sets than conventional thinking suggests. Indeed, such mind-sets qualify us as entrepreneurs, whether it be in starting, growing, or renewing our businesses.

Our contextual circumstances require us to be entrepreneurial, in that when founding a new business or division, we typically rely on internally generated funds often supplied from patient family resources. Access to this financial and, often, motivated human capital provides us with competitive advantages to overcome the liability of newness. Again, our patient capital and long-term orientation afford us the time and energy to build our business reputations over time, and that enables us to grow our enterprises. Moreover, these features have been shown to promote our investment in training, which develops the human capital to drive innovation and renewal of our businesses.

Where Three Circles Converge

After deliberating on entrepreneurship in family business for a long time, I have understood that the family business leader's entrepreneurial mind-set is best explained by integrating several frameworks that I have included in various forms throughout this book. Consider first the "classic" three-circles Venn diagram depiction of family, owners, and managers. If you place the leader, rightly, in the middle of these three circles, where they overlap, it's apparent that the leader is responsible for growing the *business,* stewarding the *family,* and creating wealth for *owners.* To achieve this involves taking risk, along with being proactive and innovative, the dimensions of entrepreneurial orientation (EO) I introduced earlier in the book.

Therefore, in EO terms, we are certainly entrepreneurs, or at least entrepreneurial. However, our entrepreneurial mind-set is multifaceted as we satisfice this tripartite of constituencies (family, owners, managers), which are, from a systems perspective, in constant flux. But in this context it's important to note something I have stressed throughout the book: that we do see ourselves as stewards with a long-term orientation.

White Board Illustration 10.1. Three, Three, Three

Therefore, if we accept—and I do—that long-term orientation is made up of resiliency, perseverance, and futurity, our entrepreneurial mind-set takes a different texture to that associated with a typical entrepreneur. I am not trying to say that nonfamily entrepreneurs are not resilient, unwilling to persevere, or lack a future orientation; but what defines our space is that we are making our entrepreneurial decisions with future generations of family members in mind.

Let's pause and take stock, using the "threes-based" graphics (White Board Illustration 10.1), to stay on top of the many interrelated ideas just introduced. Bear with any complexity, as this content really does describe the machinations of a family business leader's entrepreneurial mind-set.

In addition to the future generations of family members, our entrepreneurial decisions influence several other important constituencies: consumers, employees (the extended family), and society. As one insightful leader put it: "I want to create a business legacy. Employees and customers should be saying, 'I knew this family had a higher calling in the way they conducted business.'"

I find the messages from long-lived family companies really useful to examine. For example, consider how, when stressing the importance of their family company's target consumer, Herbert Johnson from S.C. Johnson, in his annual Profit Sharing Day speech in 1927, reminded employees about what he considered important:

> When all is said and done, this business is nothing but a symbol and when we translate this we find that it means a great many people think well of its products and that a great multitude has faith in the integrity of the men who make this product. In a very short time, the machines that are now so lively will soon become obsolete and the big buildings for all their solidarity must someday be replaced. But, a business that symbolizes can live so

long as there are human beings alive, for it is not built of such flimsy materials as steel and concrete, it is built of human opinions that may be made to live forever. The goodwill of the people is the only enduring thing in any business. It is the sole substance. . . . The rest is shadow![1]

The Entrepreneurial Skillset

If the mind-set of the family business entrepreneur is as I have positioned in White Board Illustration 10.1 earlier (and note that earlier we added a fourth trio made up of consumers/customers, employees, and society, which impact decision making), what, you must be wondering, is the *skillset* required of the family business entrepreneurial leader? Not surprisingly, I have given this, too, a lot of thought and, again, rely on some frameworks that I have stumbled on over my journey to explain it.

Ready, Willing, and Capable

In sum, what I am suggesting, again thinking in threes, is that leaders need to be ready, willing (mind-set), and capable (skillset) to contribute. Being ready and willing requires confidence, commitment, and motivation, while being capable conjures up having the requisite knowledge, skill, and experience. I recently took this one step further as I considered my role of family business leader as akin to that of someone from the medical profession who is a "specialist" in their respective field. As I sought to understand the key characteristics an effective medical specialist must demonstrate, I found—surprise, surprise—that there are *three* criteria: *skill, diligence, and judgment.* This resonates with what I need to demonstrate to my stakeholders—and with what I hope to instill in our family's next generation.

Seeing and Synthesizing Resources

When I think about skills in this context I find myself reverting to the concept of capabilities; this is fundamental to what I believe truly distinguishes family business entrepreneurs. They have the capability (i.e., the skillset) to leverage their idiosyncratic resources to understand how their business can sustain a competitive advantage. When I was effectively apprenticed to my father as I prepared to lead our business, I was laser-focused on understanding what we did differently from other businesses. And it really is that we are able to bundle our resources in a distinct way compared to others who have access, effectively, to the same resources. And this key capability, I believe, defines the skillset to lead entrepreneurially.

When I talk about this topic, people usually think that by "resources" I mean only financial resources. While those are, of course, important, it is actually much more than that. I am referring to our social capital, reputational capital, human resources (including family), physical resources, and, important, our values-centric culture. The real skill that I, and others who have mastered or are seeking to master entrepreneurial leadership, possess is the ability to understand the way past leaders have combined and integrated those resources in a way that is idiosyncratic to their family. This capability is fundamental when they pursue a strategy that best leverages their resource-driven capabilities.

To understand this fully is fundamental not only in our family business domain; all leaders face this challenge. Our difference is that we have challenges—and opportunities—that others don't. The influence of emotions, legacy, family stakeholders, and other factors can be both positive and negative. The real skillset is maximizing the positive aspects and minimizing the negative impacts of these familial dimensions as we combine the familial resources into sustainable competitive advantage.

Disrupting and Synchronizing

To grasp this whole line of thinking about entrepreneur/entrepreneurship-related topics in family business required me to take a deep dive into a collection of early literature. I did this because I was confused by the many different ways entrepreneurship and innovation are presented. Therefore, in order to really understand the role of entrepreneurs in building their own and their family firms' innovation capability, I looked closely at two approaches: Schumpeterian and Coasean. My usual disclaimer applies: this gets a bit nerdy, but it is important.

According to acclaimed economist Schumpeter (1942), the "grand poohbah" of entrepreneurship, entrepreneurship consists of introducing new products or processes of production: generating new products or reproducing old products in innovative ways. By creating novel processes and products, Schumpeter's innovator-entrepreneur disturbs the even flow of production and market, and creates profit. Specifically, by breaking from routine activity, this individual is able to generate temporary gaps between the prices of inputs and outputs. The nexus of Schumpeter's thesis is that, until imitators once again force process and cost into conformity, the innovator is able to secure real pre-profits. As such, Schumpeter's innovator acts to disturb the existing market equilibrium, initiating change that generates new opportunities. Although each burst of entrepreneurial innovation leads ultimately to a new equilibrium, the entrepreneur is presented as a *dis-equilibrating* force rather than an equilibrating one. In other words, the entrepreneur (you and I) is constantly on the lookout to disturb. This describes me to a tee.

The other approach, that of Coase (1937), introduces an alternate yet complementary explanation to Schumpeter's. Coase does not see the entrepreneur as an agent of change. Rather, Coase's coordinator-innovator is an agent of efficiency whose role is to select the optimal production mode based on the alignment of the organizational hierarchy with external market pressures. Therefore, my interpretation of these two scholars and their approaches is that they complement each other, and this is important. It is not an "either-or" approach, but a "both-and." This interpretation also resonates with my role as a leader of our family business. On one hand, I need to disturb the system, but then also I need to calm the waters to enable efficiency and alignment. Therefore, this adds to my ability to position the entrepreneurial mind-set. But I seem to be avoiding detailing the more specific *skillsets* required of an entrepreneurial family business leader. So here goes.

Technology-Driven and Business-Driven Skills

Again I went looking for an approach that resonated with my experience with this subject, emerging with the proposal that the skillset to lead entrepreneurially comprises the ability to mold and manage two (not the usual three!) separate capabilities: *technology-driven* (i.e., technology development capability and operations capability) and *business-driven* (i.e., management capability and transaction capability). Technology-driven capabilities facilitate the creation of new products and processes, while business-driven skills synchronize the integration and coordination of technology-driven capabilities. Looping back, technology-driven capabilities fall under the Schumpeterian perspective (my role as chief disturbing officer), while business-driven capabilities are associated with Coase (my role as chief synchronization officer).

Therefore, if you entertain, like I have, that an entrepreneurial leader is part Schumpeterian part Coasean, part technology (disturber) part business (synchronizer), you will likely be thirsting for more detail. I see my role as disturber (technology-driven) requiring me to build capabilities in the production function, resulting in products and services representing new technical patterns, inspirations, and breakthroughs for our business.

In addition, I need to be operationally capable. In other words, I need to be process focused. This necessitates being very nuts-and-bolts confident and includes the ability to contribute to strategic advantage by leading processes that deliver continuous cost reduction, quality improvement, strategic flexibility, and stakeholder responsiveness. Importantly, understanding this also allows me to prepare adequately the next generation of leaders.

Moreover, my leadership role as a synthesizer (business-driven) involves my managerial capability and requires taking action and responding appropriately in situations where technology fails to be perfectly routinized. In the increasingly complex and unpredictable environments we face, where, more than ever, problem-solving and decisions rely on imperfect information, management capability requires a repertoire of skills that must be applied flexibly. Management capability requires innovative responses to reduce costs resulting from uncertainty and pertains to the continual adjustment of administrative structures and the orchestration of resources. As such, this capability-slash-skillset combines continuity with innovation, which I know resonates with family business leaders across contexts.

But, in addition to this managerial capability, there is a requirement for the leader to transact, which is something that many overlook when they undertake a skillset audit on themselves. Any entrepreneur needs to *sell*. From this perspective, then, I am proposing that family business leadership and, as a consequence, sustainable advantage, is heightened for leaders who facilitate their businesses' ability to innovate via transaction capability. Why? Because the new products created through *technology* capability, produced efficiently through processes introduced via *operations* capability in a firm in which all areas of the firm are harmonized through capable *management,* will be transacted economically, with reduction of marketing, bargaining, and delivery costs.

To better depict what I consider a very good example of an entrepreneur in the Schumpeter–Coase frame and operating within the family business system, consider the story of Technigro. Technigro is a vegetation management landscaping business renowned for its award-winning research and development and industry-leading innovations, including DriftProof Sprayer, SmartWiper, EcoWash, EcoSpray, WeedBrush, and, more recently, the Safety Capsule.

Nick Bloor and Technigro: Illustrative Story

The Bloor family prides itself on espousing the values of (1) finding a better way (2) achieving more, (3) taking time to listen, and (4) doing the right thing. To enact these values their principal purpose is very much aligned with the ideas I canvased throughout this book, specifically, *to harness people, knowledge, technology, and systems—in their context—to change the way vegetation is managed forever.*

Nick's *strategy* has always been to involve family in decision making, and as such their business has always projected an EO coupled with a long-term perspective. In order to be entrepreneurial in ways that did not expose them to too much risk as an innovative business, they have always maintained close relationships with customers. They, like many like them, try to solve their problems with their innovations. This visibility with customers influences the nature and form of their innovations, as they seek to make services available in competitively advantageous ways—better, safer vegetation management at value-for-money prices.

Particular lessons learned from observing Nick as the entrepreneur leading Technigro provide guidelines for other family business operators seeking to promote innovative behavior and include:

1. his embrace of stakeholders both inside and outside of the business,
2. his long-term view,
3. as an architect, his stress on simplicity of design, which when coupled with open communication processes not only avoided many complexities but also helped to inspire an entrepreneurial culture,
4. his total commitment to learning and the refinement of his "cognitive skills,"
5. his capacity to mobilize financial and nonfinancial resources from family, and
6. the family's shared belief in the business being an extension of their family.

One way to capture what I have seen at Technigro and in many entrepreneurs in action is to adapt the Janusian two-faced model, which I have white boarded in White Board Illustration 10.2. Here I am suggesting that the two faces are that of Schumpeter and Coase: one disturbing and one synthesizing. Nick Bloor, the entrepreneurial leader at Technigro, certainly is both a disruptor and a synthesizer. He has honed his *technology-driven* (i.e., technology development capability and operations capability) and *business-driven* (i.e., management capability and transaction capability) skillsets to combine his bundle of resources idiosyncratically to create a sustainable competitive advantage.

COASIAN
"SYNTHESIZER"

SCHUMPETERIAN
"DISRUPTER"

White Board Illustration 10.2. Coase and Schumpeter

Summary

All successful entrepreneurs must complement their capacity to create newness (disruptions) with skills to produce, administer, and ultimately integrate their operations. Family business entrepreneurs must do more. Importantly, their difference stems from their need to complement these entrepreneur, architect, and governor roles with that of being a steward.

While as family business leaders we may not necessarily buy into common depictions of *the entrepreneur,* I have found it useful to interpret what I do, rather than what people think I do, to understand the importance of being an entrepreneurial leader. Perhaps unexpectedly I have found support from the early classical thinkers and am now comfortable in knowing that my entrepreneurial leader role is multifaceted: one part disruptor and one part synthesizer.

Trilogy of Lessons for Best Practice Long-Term Stewardship

Lesson 1: Family leaders *entrepreneur* differently.

Lesson 2: Patient capital and novel resource orchestration are leverageable advantages of private ownership.

Lesson 3: Interpreting and prioritizing dependent on the current and future needs of the family and the business drive the behavior of the entrepreneurial leader.

Exemplar Story: The Entrepreneur

By 2010 Family Retailer (FR) on a 38-acre site in a suburb of a major U.S. city was the largest single-store consumer electronics and appliance dealer in the nation, with over $300 million in sales, 1,000 employees, and customers from a 100-mile radius touching on four states. Even in the economic downturn of 2008 and 2009, its business sustained growth of 10 to 15 percent per year.

The sole location housed a showroom modeled after lobbies in fancy Las Vegas hotels, departments of customer service, repair, e-commerce, and installation, besides warehousing, loading docks, fleet maintenance and storage for 220 trucks, an employee cafeteria with televisions and computers, and an on-site employee gymnasium. FR's ratio of salesperson to customer was three times the industry average. Its employee retention averaged 5 years, which was 2.5 times the norm, with many workers employed there more than 20 years. Its G2 leader, the sole son in the family, described the operation: "We do everything ourselves. We have our own installers and do our own service because we've found that if we give the job to somebody else, they just don't care like we do."

The business was founded in 1936 by a wife–husband couple selling radios, using their home basement as the warehouse. They had two daughters in addition to their son. He worked in the business and eventually bought out his sisters. In 2010, at age 71, he was still active in the business and held the title of CEO. His four offspring each joined the business after college and working elsewhere for two or more years. Now aged 39 to 46, they all held the title of copresident. The eldest oversaw finance and was the company spokesperson. The second worked in customer service and human resources. The next headed up the e-commerce division. The youngest worked with advertising, merchandising, and electronics purchasing. All were married, with a total of 11 children among them.

FR had never had a board of directors, though the family CEO sought advice informally from peers when needed. He shared, "We do things quickly amongst ourselves. The process would be impossible, with too much formality and talk. The kids get their way 98 percent of the time." The offspring countered, "Dad has the final vote."

The CEO was known for his innovative merchandising. FR was the first retailer in the country to sell extremely high-end in-home theater systems. When one offspring copresident suggested a kiosk in the store for luxury watches, the CEO added it. Assuming that customers would shop longer if they could have a nice affordable place to eat nearby, he opened a sit-down restaurant named after his mother in the parking lot. In the same building as the restaurant, he built a design center, renting space to purveyors of high-end products that were complementary to items FR carried, like bathroom and kitchen fixtures.

The CEO had devised a succession plan in the event of his retirement or death. The four offspring would continue working together—but one would be named CEO, and the other three would remain copresidents. In 2010 the CEO was the only person who knew which of the four would be the successor. "The one with the eye on growth will be the anointed one," he said.

This exemplar story is based on the following case study: Lloyd Shefsky and Carol Adler Zsolnay, *Abt Electronics: Next Steps in a Parent/Sibling-Managed Family Business*, Kellogg Case #5-210-258, published 2010.

Stewart's Takeaways from the Exemplar Story: The Entrepreneur

- This entrepreneur's decisions demonstrate innovation, being proactive and risk-taking with a laser focus on customers, and initiating projects that seem counterintuitive (having only one retail location, selling watches in an appliance store; giving the store a Las Vegas makeover). They have risk-proofed the business.

- What is not yet proven is how successful the counterintuitive plan for succession will be—where only one member of the family knows who the anointed one is. What will the structure look like when the siblings are in charge without their father? Have they risk-proofed the family?

Note

1. Joe Lindner, ed. "1886–1986: One Hundred Years of Leadership," special issue, *Johnson Wax Magazine* (1986), 11.

CHAPTER ELEVEN

Synthesis, Integration, and Final Insights

> Members of [an individual's] own family, those who usually live in the same house with him, his parents, his children, his brothers and sisters, are naturally the objects of his warmest affections . . . [but] the affection gradually diminishes as the relation grows more and more remote.
>
> —Adam Smith, *Theory of Moral Sentiment,* 1759

In writing this book I set out to enlighten you about leadership of a family business. In particular, I sought to highlight why, how, and when it is different from leading a nonfamily business. For me reaching a position to share these thoughts has been a learning journey—a journey in which both *content* and *process* have been instructive. The content has been concentrated into my mind-set, complemented by a set of skills. My idiosyncratic learning process has been founded on a set of principles aimed at making sense of the mess.

The purpose of this final chapter is not to introduce new content but instead to synthesize and integrate that which has gone before, and share some further insights driven from this synthesis and integration. Throughout the previous chapters, I have sought to unpack the complex everyday world of family business leadership; in this chapter I seek to put it back together (and to further share how my thinking works; in the appendix, I include a full-blown case study that concludes with my analysis using the AGES framework).

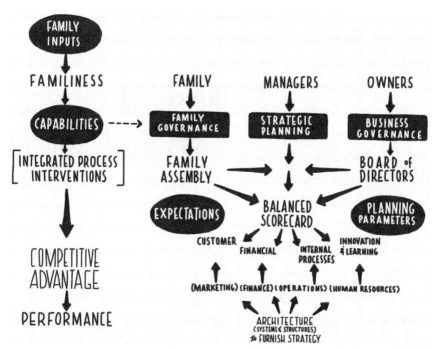

White Board Illustration 11.1. Synthesis and Integration

For now, allow me to share the white board illustration which, I think, synthesizes and integrates the key concepts introduced in the preceding chapters.

White Board Illustration 11.1 beckons further description, though I am hopeful you can follow my musings in the drawing. Effectively, what it demonstrates is that family inputs are foundational in building familiness, the resources idiosyncratic to our family business and which contribute to the capabilities from which we employ integrated process interventions to develop our competitive advantage and around which we craft our strategy to deliver superior performance. Follow the boxes and arrows along the left-hand side of the illustration as you *reread* this paragraph!

Further integration is supplied by the remainder of the boxes and arrows in the main section of the illustration. The three-circles-framework-linked drivers of family, managers, and owners at the top should be familiar to you and provide avenues for the introduction of family governance, business governance, and strategic planning, respectively. Each of these drive the structures and process that need to be reflected in the firm's architecture, which, in turn, are managed and measured by the (BSC) strategic mapping tool. I encourage you to design your own version of this boxes and arrows sketch, as it really does capture what I think is useful in helping me succinctly understand my lot. Add your voice. Make it your own. And remember, if you have seen one family business, you have seen one family business. Family businesses are all the same but different!

Now some final insights. The first insight that is now apparent to me through the process of developing this book is the awareness that leading a business family requires significant intellectual capacity. I had never really stopped to consider myself in this light. Specifically, the combination of better understanding the frameworks I have shared and the observation of others who have mastered the business family leader role has me convinced that this really is an intellectual challenge that we face.

In order to better understand this insight of mine, therefore, and capture more eloquently what the leadership mind-set is in the context of leading a family business, I ventured to find out what it meant to be "an intellectual" and discovered that, according to one source, intellectuals

- try not to overstate their confidence,
- are very conscious about where the gaps in their knowledge are and are driven to fill in those gaps,
- want to understand the world at least as much as they want to be admired,
- try to view issues from as many relevant perspectives as they can,
- are generally willing to change their minds if the evidence goes against them,
- understand how easy it is for people to fool themselves,
- take extra measures to try to avoid fooling themselves, and
- will stop and rethink things when someone they respect suggests they might be fooling themselves.

These concepts do really resonate with me and, when I get around to it, will be refined and added to my white board of concepts.

Here is another insight. Throughout the book, you can observe my preoccupation with thinking in threes. Recall the Venn diagram depictions of EO, LTO, the subdimensions of stewardship, being ready, willing and capable, the thesis, antithesis, synthesis trilogy, and then earlier the introduction of the concept of the trilemma. Whether this has its roots in the fact that I am third generation, that I am one of three in my generation, or that I have been overexposed to the three-circles framework, I can't be sure, but it seems to be omnipresent in my life. But, importantly, and this is an insight that has become more apparent through the collating of this book, thinking in threes is increasingly helping me to better understand my role as a leader.

White Board Illustration 11.2 brings this insight to life. It is currently hanging on my office wall and has helped to remind me of the complexity of my leadership role. More specifically, if I change the words from GOOD, CHEAP, FAST, to OWNERS, FAMILY, MANAGEMENT, I am able to form dyads from the triad, if that makes sense, and better make sense of how focusing on two will impact the third.

Building off the image in White Board Illustration 11.2, the three versions this insight makes me as a leader of the family and the business are as follows:

1. Focusing on OWNERS & FAMILY will potentially negatively impact MANAGERS.
2. Focusing on MANAGERS & OWNERS will potentially negatively impact FAMILY.
3. Focusing on FAMILY & MANAGERS will potentially negatively impact OWNERS.

Therefore, here's the penultimate insight: there really is no solution. There are only awareness and a commitment to continue to learn. Leading a family business is a web of paradoxes that can be at best managed, and this book has been, from the very beginning, a series of classes in Paradox School. My way of navigating the complexities of the paradoxical landscape is to embrace the many "trilogies of lessons for best practice long-term stewardship" I have included at the end of each chapter.

TO REMIND ME OF A TRILEMMA: POSTER ON MY OFFICE WALL

White Board Illustration 11.2. A Classic Trilemma

I admittedly look for ways of making the complex simple—thus my white boarding approach. I use as my compass the *ideal* situation that I frame quite simply as "continuity." But if I were to tease this out, I would suggest that the long-term future of the business, the family, and its reputation and the ability to fulfill the economic and social needs of current and future generations are all fundamental, but challenging, concerns for family business leaders.

In saying that, you will have noted how I do like to try to understand paradoxes by exploring both the mind-set and skillset required to be at my optimum, to balance my disrupting Schumpeterian with my synthesizing Coasean. I rely heavily on the stories of others and have shared only a few who have taught me what I know. I look to frameworks and evidence; perhaps that *is* the intellectual in me, to make sense of the mess that really is our world where family, ownership, and management systems are simultaneously independent and interdependent.

And my final insight that this book project has reinforced is the importance to continue to find novel ways to communicate my story and share my ideas and ideals. For me, the single most important management tool is a white board to capture thoughts, to map complex relationships, and make the complex simple. If you don't have one in your office, paint one of your walls with white board paint, or write on the windows. It is how we learned to learn as children, and it will never go out of fashion.

Enjoy the journey, and *respect the challenge.*

Stewart "Lead On" Macduff

Dempsey Boats Case

AGES Framework Lessons Applied

Many years ago, my father had a chance meeting with an Australian business owner at an airport. Dad and Bruce Dempsey hit it off immediately, especially when my father, a passionate boat owner, learned that Bruce made boats. It was not long before the friendship turned into a commercial relationship. Shortly after their meeting my father traveled "down under" to take delivery of his newly acquired craft made carefully by Bruce. This chance beginning turned into a strong friendship, and Mum and Dad often met up with Bruce and Jenny. Over the years I met the Dempsey family, but it was not until Anthony and I joined the same MBA cohort that I learned a little more of their business operation. He selected finance classes, while I took a few electives in family business.

Therefore, when Bruce suddenly passed away, we were informed immediately. It did not take long for Anthony and his mum, knowing my interest in family business matters, to approach me regarding what they should do now that Bruce had passed away. The family could put the business on the market, but with Anthony and his older brother Tim working in the business, their preference was to continue owning and operating the business. They were keen to know if the business could be made great again.

Given I had some leave due, I took a flight down to Australia to help the Dempsey family. To give you greater context, what follows is a description of the Dempsey family and their business. I follow this by my analysis of the situation, using the AGES framework.

Descriptive Details: Dempsey Boats and Dempsey Family

Bruce had been passionate about boats from a very early age, at first building small models and replicas before he began designing and building full-size vessels in his late teens. He founded Dempsey Boats Pty Ltd in 1958 after completing an apprenticeship with a large shipbuilder in Geelong. Bruce designed and built just six power boats in that year—handmade vessels all less than five meters in length. These boats were beautifully crafted, and the focus was on creating a comfortable and efficient hull suitable for regular recreational boating.

From this point forward, Dempsey Boats experienced sustained growth. Through Bruce's exacting standards, focus on quality, and best-practice manufacturing, Dempsey Boats is now one of Australia's largest fiberglass recreational boat builders. The company employs 42 staff with a turnover of approximately $18 million.

Dempsey Boats is in many ways a typical Australian family business. Bruce's wife, Jenny, supported him throughout the 50-year history of the firm, and his two sons, Tim and Anthony, both work in the firm. His daughter Leah has a successful career outside the business but remains very close to the family.

The Boat Building Industry

The Australian recreational boat building industry is a mature market with several large manufacturers and a number of small niche market-driven companies located around the country. Dempsey Boats is one of the dominant manufacturers in the high-end fiberglass boat niche market.

The boat building industry in Australia had revenues of $1.5 billion in 2008, growing by 5.3 percent over the previous year. The industry had close to 2,000 manufacturing enterprises in 2008 and supported 7,900 employees.

Most manufacturers are situated in large coastal cities, with major operations located in Melbourne, Sydney, and Hobart, as well as a growing number on Queensland's Gold Coast.

Recreational boats are largely a discretionary purchase, and sales are therefore strongly affected by the overall state of the economy. As such, the industry, and particularly the recreational component, is somewhat cyclical. However, as a family-owned private company, Dempsey Boats has been able to weather half a century of economic cycles with its "traditional" sales strategy, conservative attitude to debt, strong reliance on stakeholder relationships, and patient capital approach.

The Company

Now headquartered in Melbourne, Victoria, Dempsey Boats was founded by Bruce Dempsey in 1958. The company's major manufacturing plant is also located in Melbourne, with a number of interstate agents, who sell on consignment, located along the Eastern seaboard. Dempsey Boats manufactures around 150 hand-laid fiberglass boats each year across a range of models, primarily for the recreational market. Although changing from timber to fiberglass boats with the technological advancements, the company's unique hull design has stood the test of time for over 50 years.

Total revenues for 2009 were just under $18 million, with a net profit of approximately $650,000 (Tables A.1–A.3 show full financial data for Dempsey Boats over the last three to five years).

Dempsey Boats has built and maintained a reputation for quality products with a brand well recognized in the marketplace. Bruce was the driving force behind this commitment. Employees are acutely aware of Bruce's standing in the industry, and he was well respected by all. Similarly, customers respond favorably to the family-based brand, which Dempsey Boats has developed and actively promoted.

Bruce was committed to research and development, spending over $500,000 each year on these activities (including salaries). The company has a number of patented designs, such as anti-fouling coatings and their unique hull, which are very popular in the recreational market. Although Bruce was heavily involved in developing many of these products, major responsibility for the design function is now in the hands of his son Tim.

With recent growth, Dempsey Boats reached a point in its life cycle that necessitated the introduction of professional management practices. Recognizing this, in 2007, Bruce removed himself from the position of CEO (remaining as chairman of the board) and hired a nonfamily manager to replace him. While the new CEO had made some efforts to professionalize the management and governance of the firm, Bruce's influence had prevented widespread changes from occurring.

In terms of ownership, in 2007 a private investor bought a 30 percent share of Dempsey Boats. Of the remaining 70 percent, the founding generation owned 31 percent, while each of the three children held 13 percent of the company and were entitled to dividends and voting rights commensurate with their shareholding.

The individual private investor contribution was instigated by Bruce to enable the family to liquidate some of its wealth locked up in the business. As he got older he realized that although the family had always lived well, their wealth was constantly reinvested in the business, and little cash was available for retirement. A private equity fund investment had been recommended by his friends as a means of freeing up some cash for the family; however, Bruce found the individual private investor option much more palatable.

As a condition of the deal, the private investor required Dempsey Boats to have a board of directors, which included the investor as a board member. Bruce hastily appointed his two sons as directors, along with two other executives, one of whom was his close ally, to make sure Dempsey Boats complied with this requirement. No one, including Bruce, was entirely sure of their role in this capacity, particularly as board meetings were run as just another business meeting.

Although the individual private investment contribution eroded the family's ownership, it allowed Dempsey Boats to continue to sustain growth and stay at the cutting edge of world's best practice, while still facilitating the potential to expand.

Bruce was reluctant to change his selling strategy practices, which had served him well. He still preferred to have finished boats in showrooms around the country, where consumers could see the uniqueness and classic finish of his boats. Agents would sell these Dempsey Boats under a consignment selling model. This showroom stock tied up a large amount of capital, and Anthony strongly encouraged his father to change to a more conventional sales model, including now widely accepted commerce practices. As was the norm, Tim sided with his father, as this was how Tim had always seen the industry work. Reluctant to change his business model, Bruce preferred to pursue an external injection of capital by selling 30 percent of the business to a private investor.

The Family and the Business

As a number of family members hold key positions within the company, many stakeholders consider the firm to be a family business. Despite this, little attention had ever been given to succession planning. Prior to his unexpected death, Bruce, though employing a CEO external to the family, and introducing a board of directors, was reluctant to relinquish his influence over the business.

Bruce's two sons grew up surrounded by boat building, spending many afternoons and school holidays in the boat factory environment. It was inevitable they would both end up working in the business, although this came about in different ways for each of the boys.

Tim, the eldest son, left school at 15 to join his father in the business, working on the factory floor and learning the business from the ground up. Like his father, Tim was passionate about boat building and became heavily involved in developing new products and improving existing hull designs. Bruce required Tim to undertake a formal training course as a shipwright. Tim's creativity was put to good use at Dempsey Boats, and at age 25 he took responsibility for the company's designs.

Tim married at age 21 and had two daughters with his first wife, Jane. However, the marriage soon broke down and the pair was divorced by the time Tim was 27. Tim was upset by the divorce, but he remarried and had a son (Bruce Dempsey, Jr., 17) with his second wife, Tiffany.

Bruce's younger son Anthony joined the business with a different skillset and training. A natural learner, Anthony received a full scholarship to a prestigious Melbourne private school. After leaving school, he studied accounting and finance at Melbourne University. A high academic achiever, he took a postgraduate job with a large accounting firm in the city. It wasn't until 10 years later that Anthony realized that he could play an important role in the family business. By this time, he had also completed an MBA in the United States. Anthony married an American, Laura, whom he met while studying his MBA. They have no children.

Anthony's experience and proven track record outside Dempsey Boats resulted in his appointment to the position of CFO when he decided to join the business. This caused some tension with his older brother, who had spent so long working in the firm. Tim felt Anthony did not understand the business in the same way that he did and was initially skeptical about Anthony's motives in joining.

Leah, Bruce's youngest child (and only daughter), never had any interest in joining the family business. She studied fine arts at university before moving to France to work in various art galleries. Leah married a Frenchman, Jacques, and has since returned to live in Sydney with their three children.

A number of key nonfamily staff are also integral to Dempsey Boats; many of them have been with the company for a long time. The current CEO, Mark Best, was appointed to the position in 2007. Mark came from a top management position in a large Sydney-based luxury boat manufacturer. There was some initial conflict between Bruce and Mark, but over time Mark became accustomed to the culture of this family firm and mostly took direction from Bruce as founding chairman of the company.

Chief operating officer (COO) Malcolm Rann has been with Dempsey Boats for over 25 years and was originally an engineering consultant to the business. Bruce and Malcolm had always been good friends, with a strong working relationship that added substantial value to the business.

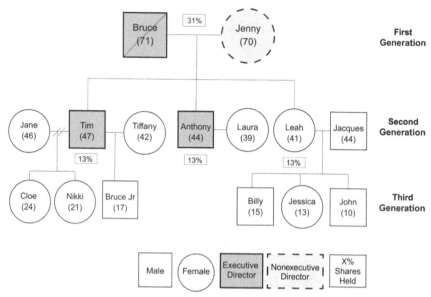

Diagram A.1   Dempsey Boats Family Genogram

Source: Moores, K., & Craig, J. B. (2015). *The Dempsey family case. Family Business Casebook.* J. Astrachan and T. Pieper (Ed.). Kennesaw State University Publishing.

Malcolm's practical, can-do attitude complemented Bruce's dominant, outgoing entrepreneurial style. The COO position evolved due to Malcolm's knowledge of the business and his working rapport and trust with Bruce.

Prior to Bruce's death, there were seven directors on the company's board of directors: Bruce and his two sons Tim and Anthony, Mark (CEO), Malcolm (COO), and private investor John Eastlake, whose board membership was a requirement of his original investment deal. Bruce's wife Jenny is also a director of the company, although she does not attend the meetings and has limited knowledge of day-to-day operations.

Board meetings are usually held four times per year, with Anthony, Mark, and Malcolm presenting management reports. However, the timing and structure of meetings are reasonably ad hoc, with very little preparation undertaken. Board papers are hastily prepared, disorganized, and distributed late, much to the frustration of John, the only external director. Further hampering the board process is the constant discussion of family issues, which draw attention away from important business issues.

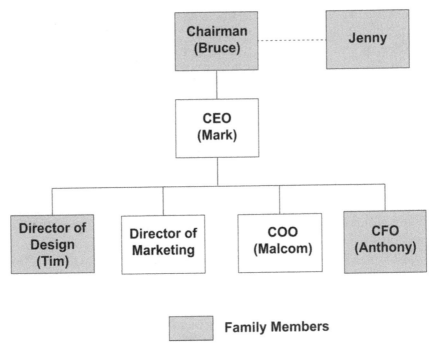

Family Members

Diagram A.2   Dempsey Boats Senior Management Structure

Risk management is particularly poorly addressed by the board. There are no clear risk-management guidelines or policies in place, and Mark, John, and Anthony feel as though the company virtually ignores many contemporary risks that have the potential to do substantial damage to the business.

Bruce dominated these board meetings as chairman, and, like Mark, the other directors tended to follow his lead rather than causing any arguments. After all, he had run the company for over 50 years. Anthony was increasingly frustrated with the lack of strategic direction and was beginning to question his decision to join the family business.

A short time ago Leah expressed concern to her father about the equality of distribution of benefits and rewards from the family business. She was especially perturbed by the apparent superior living standard of her brothers and their families' relative to her own family which, since her return to Australia, was relatively basic due to her husband's struggle to establish himself in the local art community. Her father assured her that he would attend to this and, true to his word, raised the matter at a recent board meeting under the topic of "other business." Bruce spoke about how he wanted to treat all his children equally, but what ensued was an extended and heated discussion between Bruce and his two sons. John Eastlake sat by, somewhat taken aback by the highly emotional exchange. Finally, Bruce ended the matter by abruptly declaring the board meeting closed, with the pronouncement "I will take care of this matter." Now, though Leah was naturally grieving the loss of her father, she was wondering who would represent her interests in the family business.

The Future

On the Monday following Bruce's death, the board members held an emergency meeting to discuss the future of Dempsey Boats. As with any family business, there were many issues to be discussed, most of them emotionally charged by the close overlap of family and business.

Primary among the issues for discussion was a replacement for Bruce as chairman of the board. So many elements of the business relied on Bruce's input, making it potentially harmful to leave this role vacant. Bruce had not made his intentions clear in relation to succession, further complicating the replacement decision.

The other board members were aware of the underlying rivalry between Bruce's two sons. Perhaps Bruce had not nominated one of them as a successor to avoid the damage this rivalry could potentially do to the business, or maybe his intention was to spark healthy competition between his sons. Either way, the current situation had intensified these feelings, and it was obvious that each brother considered himself worthy to be the chairman.

However, there were other potential candidates for the position. Malcolm Rann had a comprehensive understanding of the entire company and significant experience working alongside Bruce. Perhaps he was better placed to fill the role of chairman. CEO Mark Best was also an option, given his broad-reaching, albeit relatively short-lived, position and experience.

Although there was uncertainty about who would be chosen as Bruce's formal successor, there was one thing that everybody agreed upon: Dempsey Boats needed major professionalization.

CEO Mark Best

While he had some tense disagreements with Bruce when he first took the CEO position, with Bruce's passing, Mark Best now better understood his role as a nonfamily executive and the importance of the business to Bruce and his family. Family and business systems were truly intertwined.

The overlap of these two systems meant that Bruce's death had the potential to be disastrous for the company. Mark was particularly concerned that the internal problems in the business could overshadow important external issues facing Dempsey Boats. It was these external issues that could most rapidly damage the business, and Mark knew it was his responsibility to ensure these were not overlooked.

On a personal level, Mark believed he had the ability to lead the firm successfully into the future, but he was unsure whether employees and family members would place sufficient confidence in him to do this effectively. He had certainly been overruled by family members in the past.

Moreover, Mark's background in marine-related industries had led him to develop a particular concern for environmental issues. He had investigated Dempsey Boats thoroughly before he took on the role, finding it to be a good corporate citizen with a strong environmental track record. However, recent changes to the manufacturing process at both the fiberglass laying and finishing stages were causing Mark some concern. To maintain their environment-friendly position, a new waste-management system was necessary as part of an upgrade to the company's manufacturing facility.

This required a critical decision from the board regarding which waste-management system to invest in. One option involved the purchase of a relatively cheap machine that utilized the factory's existing waste-management system. The alternative was the purchase of a more expensive machine that required an overhaul of the existing waste-management system to meet the supplier's requirements.

To Mark, the choice was clear: the extra spending was necessary to maintain the company's reputation as a quality producer and to ensure it was a leader in the area of environmental management. Anthony supported Mark on this. However, Bruce, who had become more conservative and less innovative as he grew older—and Tim—had disagreed with this notion, preferring to save money and continue with the factory's already stretched waste-management system.

Mark believed the company was glossing over a decision which may generate a negative response from their increasingly environmentally conscious consumers.

Private Investor John Eastlake

John Eastlake had been an avid Dempsey Boat fan for a long time, having owned a number of their craft. Although John is an experienced and successful investor, when the opportunity for investment in Dempsey

Boats arose, the decision was a relatively emotional one, which lacked thorough investigation into the company. John's investment style is to buy into a firm, have a strong input into the organization, and then sell within a predetermined time (usually between 6 and 10 years) at an expected profit.

John had become increasingly frustrated in his role since investing and taking up directorship at Dempsey Boats two-and-a-half years ago. One of his objectives when joining the board was to develop a long-range strategic plan and provide clear direction for the future of the business—something that was lacking before his investment.

The hiring of CEO Mark Best shortly after John's involvement in Dempsey Boats began made John's task somewhat easier; he now had someone else in the boardroom with an external, corporate background. John liked Mark but was not sure of his ability to lead the business in Bruce's absence. The leadership gap left by Bruce would be a difficult one to fill, and he was sure that uncertain times lay ahead.

John was particularly concerned about the managerial and leadership capabilities of Bruce's two sons. They had both begun to raise their interest in running the business, and he feared that they would feel entitled to step into Bruce's shoes following his untimely death. This forthcoming competition for the chairmanship would no doubt further distract Dempsey Boats from the strategic planning efforts John had been working toward.

The lack of strategic focus meant that Dempsey Boats was missing opportunities taken up by competitors. John believed potential openings in new markets were not being pursued, while overinvestment was occurring in existing markets where there was less opportunity for growth. Significant competitive pressures were coming from south-east Queensland, where strong growth in boat-building activity was moving the center of gravity away from Sydney and Melbourne. In addition, while significant funds were expended at Dempsey Boats on research and development, poor implementation was hampering potential returns.

John was also concerned about developing an exit strategy for his investment. He needed the business in shape to make it attractive to potential buyers, as his investment horizon on this project was about six years. For this to happen, John needed the board to function more like a board should; and for the board to be less family dominated. A good example of this need was highlighted when a recent generous dividend payout was approved—a payout that he voted against in the interest of growing the value of the firm. He was overruled by family directors.

John was not interested in being involved in operations—he took his directorship to be a strategic-level role. Although he was never entirely happy with the board arrangement when Bruce Dempsey was around, a poor replacement could do more damage to the business at an operational level. As John considered his options, he knew timing was critical: appropriate interventions may avoid negative impact of Bruce's death on the business.

John planned to discuss his thoughts informally with the other board members and senior management. He knew his actions may well determine the future of Dempsey Boats.

The Family

The Daughter—Leah Dupont (nee Dempsey)

There is no doubt that Leah's perspectives on the business differed from those of her older brothers. She chose not to work in the business, as her interests lay elsewhere. After university she lived in France for eight years, working in a number of art galleries in and around Paris. It was during this time that she married a French artist, Jacques Dupont. However, she found herself longing to come back to Australia and eventually returned to Sydney, where she has lived with her husband for almost five years.

Despite these outside interests, Leah had always remained close to her family, and conversations inevitably included the latest happenings at Dempsey Boats. She also received annual dividends in respect of her ownership in the company. However, these dividends were somewhat erratic and seemed to be determined by Bruce alone, based on his sentiments at the time.

Bruce's sudden death made Leah realize just how little she knew about the business, particularly when it came to the company's strategic direction and overall financial situation. She felt that as a shareholder and family member, she needed more engagement with the family business without getting involved in its day-to-day operations. This need for engagement was particularly pertinent given the uncertainty surrounding the future of the business, and the need for family and shareholder input in determining what this future may look like.

Specifically, Leah felt that it was important to maintain fairness among family members, particularly between herself and her brothers. Given they were contributing far more to the business than she was, Leah thought it would be wise to have transparent mechanisms in place to determine who should get what out of the business.

Leah knew these were all sensitive issues requiring a careful approach. She was well aware that the current environment was conducive to tension among family members, and she had no intention of breaking down what had always been good relationships with her mother and brothers. She felt that, where possible, family issues should be separated from business issues—and distinct forums were needed for such issues to be discussed.

If the second-generation members could effectively work through this difficult time in a way that promoted the long-term success of the firm, Leah was confident that third-generation members would be more likely to show interest in continuing the family business. Now was the time to ensure that such transgenerational continuity was an option.

The Sons—Tim and Anthony

There had been tension between the two brothers since an early age, each having different personalities and interests. Tim was a gifted athlete and very popular at school, while Anthony excelled in academics and kept more to himself. This rivalry ceased when they passed their teenage years and went down separate career paths. When Anthony decided to rejoin the business, the tension flared again.

Anthony came to Dempsey Boats with many contemporary business strategies he wished to integrate into the company, having learnt them throughout his study and his work in the corporate business sector.

While Bruce was alive and dominating the board, Anthony knew many of his ideas would not be thoroughly discussed and debated at a board level. Therefore, he often refrained even from raising them. Now his father was no longer alive, and Anthony had great visions for the company. Many of these were shared by the CEO, Mark, as they had similar backgrounds and experience outside the company.

Conversely, having worked his entire career at Dempsey Boats with a design/production focus, Tim had little experience of strategic processes or how they could improve the business. He preferred to continue in the same mold as his father and stay with proven approaches the company had used since inception. Like his father, Tim was very reluctant to change.

Apart from the fact that each brother believed they deserved to be the successor of their late father as chairman, a major issue was their different strategic emphasis. Anthony wished growth for the company; Tim wished to consolidate the company's position as a leader in their niche market.

The Widow—Jenny

With her husband Bruce no longer around, Jenny was concerned about the position she had been left in. Owning 31 percent of the company, Jenny was now faced with considerable business responsibility, something she had always left to Bruce, whom she supported completely.

Jenny knew that some of the forthcoming decisions would create conflict between her children and perhaps herself. In the past Jenny had the position of "chief emotional officer" within the family, making sure each member separated his or her business-related feelings from his or her family relationships. She desperately wanted her new role to not affect the trust and relationships she had built.

My Analysis

Whenever I am asked to help colleagues with their business, I adopt an approach somewhat inspired by the medical profession—I always seek to describe the condition of the business before ever tendering any prescription. I first gather description of the business in a variety of ways that include directly observing for myself what appears to be going on in day-to-day operations. I then augment these observations with reviews of relevant documents that include strategic plans, financial statements, organization charts, and even company constitutions. These descriptions are enriched further by talking to people whether by way of formal/informal interview or in some cases survey responses. In the case of family businesses, I supplement these descriptions of the business with details of the family and their relationship to the business. These family details are best summarized in terms of a genogram and knowledge of ownership details of the business. I always know where family are employed in the business and if they occupy seats on the board. I usually discover that there is little, if any, form of family governance in place.

I then seek to make some sense of these rich descriptions by classifying them—I put them into "boxes" using some of the frames outlined in the chapters of this book. For example, I would often try to identify what life stage the business is at in terms of being in start-up, growth, maturity, or renewal stages. This, coupled with knowledge of the family ownership being a sibling partnership or the more complex cousin consortium, is very useful starting descriptions that enable me to advance to what I call "classified descriptions." Positioning the family business in stages of family involvement, ownership, and development helps me grasp the level of sophistication the family has installed in the form of architecture (A), governance (G), entrepreneurship (E), and stewardship (S).

Having established where the family business is at in these terms then allows me to rely on evidence-based recommendations as prescriptions to remedy any apparent "illness" in the family business. As noted earlier, this approach emulates that adopted in medicine whereby following rich descriptions of a patient's conditions (sometimes substantiated by tests, X-rays, etc.) a doctor can rely on medical science to prescribe interventions (drugs, surgery, etc.) to alleviate patient conditions.

My approach to a review of any family business usually starts at an organizational level (AGES). Then I (SAGE) make recommendations of interventions that are evidence-based best practices associated with the long-term stewardship that characterizes family firms. Depending on the circumstances, these could be driven by any or all the structures and processes (A and G) and behaviors (E and S) that are salient for the family business in question. For me there is no set sequence of looking first at architecture (A), then governance (G), and so on, because I view each business and family somewhat holistically. Much depends on how the descriptive details come to me. But if I was to offer advice on how to proceed, I would suggest that the low-hanging fruit is typically in architecture—examine the structures and systems in place that hopefully support the underlying strategy. This usually takes me quickly to who is deciding many of these things, namely the board, and I enquire as to what type of "board" it is. Sadly, I often find what is described to me as a board (of directors) turns out to be a management meeting focused always exclusively on day-to-day operations.

Architecture

When I reflected on the descriptions I gleaned of Dempsey as highlighted in the comments earlier, I saw there clearly is room to improve the architecture of the company. As was noted with recent growth, Dempsey Boats reached a point in its life cycle that necessitated the introduction of professional management practices. To effect these systems changes, Bruce made some structural adjustments, in that he appointed a nonfamily CEO and stepped back to the role of executive chairman. However, much of this appears to have been "on paper" only. The significant dimensions of "structure" relate to the structuring of activities and the structuring of authority. While Bruce appears to have shed some activities to the new CEO, his inability to delegate authority to the CEO apparently prevented widespread changes from occurring. The recent passing of Bruce may well provide both the opportunity and incentive to introduce these system changes through structural empowerment of the CEO. The bedrock for any structural changes and systems modifications will be the family's values, vision, and expectations, as developed here.

As owners, I recommend the Dempsey family test the capabilities of the CEO.

The nature and form of these changes should, however, be to support the underlying strategy. Sadly, despite the recent best efforts of private investor John Eastlake, the business does not appear to be operating under an agreed-to strategic plan. Sure, they have a selling strategy that seems to have been what served Bruce well in the past. But as Anthony has pointed out, showroom stock under this consignment approach tied up a large amount of capital, so he strongly encouraged his father to change to a more conventional sales model, including now widely accepted commerce practices. However, Bruce's reluctance to embrace the paradox of continuing differently has bedeviled Dempsey Boats over recent years.

Any hope that Dempsey could recapture its competitive advantage will depend heavily on developing a strategic plan, and I strongly urge the family to embark on a strategic planning journey as a matter of urgency. After all, strategy does matter, as does having performance systems that count the achievement of strategic goals. It will be imperative that the Dempseys jettison their old habits and embrace flexibility in developing their capabilities for growth.

Governance

To craft such a plan requires a functioning board informed by the commercially real expectations of the owners. In short, to formulate a strategic plan will require best-practice governance structures and processes to be installed: governance in both family and the business, and then the integration of both these, unlike what is currently in place, where the one board deals with both business and family matters and which appears to have been heavily dominated by Bruce.

I strongly recommend the establishment of a program of family meetings. In our experience, and those of family business friends who have taken this learning journey, these meetings are most effective when externally facilitated. Choosing an external facilitator is a crucial decision that must be taken carefully and preferably involve as many family members as possible. Merely any business facilitator or family therapist will not do. It works best when the facilitator chosen knows the family business space inside out.

Essentially these family business facilitators focus on three aspects: awareness, language, and framing. They typically make family participants aware of fundamental family business issues, highlight the risks of inaction, focus on the task at hand, and emphasize the only real option. Specifically, this entails sharing the information about the odds of continuity, breaking past the denial and procrastination that frequently paralyze the leadership of business families, defining the challenge ahead and establishing the family's readiness to meet these challenges, and stressing the necessity to manage the change process needed.

Introducing the language and terms of family business (e.g., what does stewardship mean?) helps facilitate efficient conversations that remain focused on issues at hand rather than being diverted to explain terms. Not only does this help the family to problem-solve collectively, but it does by enabling them to frame the problems and issues at hand. In this way, facilitators encourage not only learning from the past but also how to create your future by framing unrealized possibilities that can overcome the overwhelming challenges associated with governance, leadership, management, financial, and interpersonal issues. They highlight possible destinations and, importantly, pathways to reach these destinations.

Using educational interventions in this way, these facilitators will develop communication within the Dempsey family to quickly establish the family's values and a shared vision for the future. From these I would strongly recommend that the Dempseys articulate their financial and nonfinancial expectations of the business. These values, vision, and expectations will then form the cornerstones for the formulation of a business strategic plan that can be developed as a joint enterprise between the board and the Dempsey Boats executive management team.

In the context of these family meetings, not only will communication between family members be strengthened, but also these conversations can serve to educate family members about the realities of the business. In particular, mother Jenny and daughter Leah will be able to use these family meetings to develop their capabilities as active owners of the business. Third-generation family members (owners in waiting) should also be encouraged to participate in these family meetings.

Given her concern for third-generation members and their likelihood of showing interest in continuing the family business, Leah should be considered as someone to champion stewardship within the family, and she could evolve into the chair of the family council in the near term.

With family governance in place, best practice dictates that there needs to be communication between this forum of family owners and those that represent their interests as directors of the business. Business governors need to invest time in understanding the aforementioned expectations that active family owners have for the business. Populating the board of Dempsey Boats, therefore, hinges on appointing not only those fit for purpose to turn the business back to a position of sustainable competitive advantage but also those sensitive to the needs of family owners. When assured appointed governors have mind-sets that respect family owners and have skills to discharge commercial responsibilities on behalf of owners, family members are often more inclined to accept that they do not necessarily have to have a seat on the board.

At this point I am not able to recommend specific appointments for the Dempsey Boats board, but what I would strongly encourage them to consider is the appointment of a couple of external independent directors: appointees that can bring both an independence of thought and a respect for accountability. Their independence of thought is crucial, as it enables governors to garner unbiased objective views that will typically be informed by their background and experience. Their respect for accountability will manifest both up and down. They will listen to, and understand, family owners and their expectations and seek to be accountable for delivery of those expectations. With strategic plans in place they will oversee the development of architecture (structures and systems) to implement strategies and to hold management accountable for performance outcomes. Furthermore, evidence shows that external directors generally increase the work of the board while encouraging greater cohesion.

In the near term, I would encourage Jenny and her family to recommend more regular board meetings until such time as the backlog of best practices is addressed. Then, with the hosting of regular family meetings, business governance could revert to less regular meetings provided both forms of governance remain integrated.

Entrepreneurship

Fortunately, Bruce Dempsey was an acknowledged entrepreneur and over the years tried to maintain that through investing significantly in a program of research and development to drive innovations. A consequence of this is that the company has a number of patented designs that have proved very popular in the recreational market. Responsibility for these innovations has recently fallen to Tim.

The board will need to back Tim in these responsibilities by reinforcing that while the company may value its heritage it continues to embrace innovation and change in ways that Bruce always did. Investing significant sums into research and development accompanied by a long-term patient attitude to returns may well be needed to rebuild the competitive value of Dempsey. This will require courage and commitment of the business leaders. A challenging dynamic is likely to emerge in the boardroom, with private investor John Eastlake committed to an exit within the next few years.

I strongly urge the family to use the sad passing of Bruce as the catalyst to commit to an entrepreneurial path—a pathway in which to ensure that Bruce's legacy of innovation is maintained by proactively pursuing new opportunities for growth through the commercialization of their research and development initiatives. The risks involved in taking this path will need to be carefully monitored by the board in accordance with the family's tolerance for risk and their willingness to assume debt levels to finance growth in this way.

To ensure that the spirit of entrepreneurialism pervades Dempsey generations, I would also encourage those championing and leading family governance to include education sessions aimed at both respecting the legacy of the past achievements and instilling a spirit for innovation and change.

Stewardship

As noted frequently in this book, this mind-set is arguably the defining differentiator of a genuine family business. From what I gleaned from the family, there has been little conversation regarding this matter. Therefore, there has been little, if any, evidence of steward-like behaviors to date. This is not unusual, especially in families-in-business that have not installed family governance processes. After all, that is where my family gets to talk about the long term and the interests of the next and subsequent generations. We reveal our preferences through open dialogue. Therefore, unless the Dempseys are an especially chatty family, which I doubt, they, like we have, will benefit from the creation of a structure and process to stimulate these conversations.

The recommendations mentioned earlier for regular family meetings will therefore enable them to focus on building a multigenerational legacy, a legacy in which they accept the responsibility of long-term social and economic value creation. This mind-set will allow them, as a family, to embrace an obligation to generate returns to a wider group of stakeholders. In a conversation I had with Leah when I first arrived in Australia, despite her immediate self-interested concerns for equal treatment with her brothers, she did reveal concern for the next generation. In this I detect the seeds of a steward that could be nurtured over time. As recommended earlier, if she was to be encouraged and supported in the role of family council chair with the help of a seasoned family business advisor, she could emerge as the real CEO—chief emotional officer—of Dempsey Boats.

SAGE Framework

Not being a leader within the Dempsey family or its business, I have sought to act out my steward, architect, governor, and entrepreneur roles through a series of recommendations. These recommendations inform my everyday role as a leader in our family business. They are aimed at installing best practices within Dempsey Boats: best practices that have been shown to stimulate long-term stewardship.

Table A.1 Dempsey Boats Income Statement (in thousands of dollars)

	2009	2008	2007	2006	2005
Revenues	$17,799	$16,872	$16,068	$15,450	$15,000
Expenses					
Cost of goods sold	$13,260	$12,586	$12,002	$11,541	$11,220
R&D costs	$570	$540	$514	$479	$450
Marketing and administration	$2,777	$2,632	$2,507	$2,395	$2,310
Interest expense	$142	$135	$145	$154	$135
Total	$16,749	$15,893	$15,168	$14,569	$14,115
Earnings before tax	$1,050	$979	$900	$881	$885
Tax expense	$415	$387	$356	$357	$367
Net income	$635	$592	$544	$524	$518

Source: Moores, K., & Craig, J. B. (2015). *The Dempsey family case. Family Business Casebook.* J. Astrachan and T. Pieper (Ed.). Kennesaw State University Publishing.

Table A.2 Dempsey Boats Balance Sheet (in thousands of dollars)

	2009	2008	2007
Assets			
Cash	$142	$143	$136
Accounts receivable	$1,895	$1,778	$1,688
Inventory	$1,855	$1,723	$1,842
Prepaid expenses	$346	$328	$312
Total current assets	$4,238	$3,972	$3,978
Land	$266	$252	$223
Buildings	$1,608	$1,608	$1,396
Machinery and equipment	$3,001	$2,789	$2,176
Less: accumulated depreciation	−$2,121	−$1,997	−$1,732
Other assets	$855	$914	$693
Total noncurrent assets	$3,609	$3,566	$2,756
Total assets	$7,847	$7,538	$6,734

(continued)

Table A.2 (*continued*)

	2009	2008	2007
Liabilities			
Notes payable	$569	$528	$607
Trade accounts payable	$1,112	$1,137	$1,279
Accrued liabilities	$1,154	$1,239	$1,366
Tax payable	$176	$200	$179
Current portion of long-term debt	$18	$23	$22
Total current liabilities	$3,029	$3,127	$3,453
Long-term debt	$364	$408	$509
Obligations under capital lease	$77	$75	$77
Deferred tax	$134	$138	$125
Deferred liabilities	$207	$180	$150
Total noncurrent liabilities	$782	$801	$861
Total liabilities	$3,811	$3,928	$4,314
Shareholders' equity			
Share capital	$2,457	$2,457	$1,644
Retained earnings	$1,579	$1,153	$776
Total shareholders' equity	$4,036	$3,610	$2,420

Source: Moores, K., & Craig, J. B. (2015). *The Dempsey family case. Family Business Casebook.* J. Astrachan and T. Pieper (Ed.). Kennesaw State University Publishing.

Table A.3 Dempsey Boats Cash Flow Statement (in thousands of dollars)

	2009	2008	2007
Operating activities			
Net income	635	592	544
Depreciation and amortization	266	265	230
Adjustment for deferred taxes	−4	14	−8
	897	871	766
Adjustments for			
Change in receivables	−118	−89	−137
Change in inventories	−133	119	−139
Change in accounts payable	−24	−143	30
Change in accrued taxes	−24	20	13
Change in other current assets	−18	−16	8
Change in other current liabilities	−90	−126	−85
	−407	−235	−310
Cash flow—operations	490	636	456

Investing activities			
Net additions to property, plant, and equipment	−369	−854	−290
Increase in other assets	59	−221	−49
Cash flow—investing	−310	−1075	−339
Financing activities			
Change in notes payable	41	−80	−24
Change in long-term debt	−43	−101	23
Change in capital lease	2	−2	8
Change in other liabilities	28	30	52
Cash dividends paid	−209	−215	−185
Sale of shares	0	814	0
Cash flow—financing	−181	446	−126
Increase (decrease) in cash	−1	7	−9
Cash and equivalents, January 1	43	36	45
Cash and equivalents, December 31	42	43	36

Source: Moores, K., & Craig, J. B. (2015). *The Dempsey family case. Family Business Casebook.* J. Astrachan and T. Pieper (Ed.). Kennesaw State University Publishing.

Recommended Further Reading

Chapter 1: Introducing Stewart Macduff

Gosling, J., & Mintzberg, H. (2003). The five minds of a manager. *Harvard Business Review, 81*(11), 54–63.

Handy, C. (1995). *The age of paradox*. Harvard Business Press.

Handy, C. (2011). *The empty raincoat: Making sense of the future*. Random House.

Moores, K., & Barrett, M. (2003). *Learning family business: Paradoxes and pathways*. (2002) Ashgate Publishing Limited. Reprinted (2010) Bond University Press.

Peltier, J. W., Hay, A., & Drago, W. (2005). The reflective learning continuum: Reflecting on reflection. *Journal of Marketing Education, 27*(3), 250–263.

Schuman, A., Stutz, S., & Ward, J. (2010). *Family business as paradox*. Springer.

Chapter 2: Architecture

Chandler, A. D. (1990). *Strategy and structure: Chapters in the history of the industrial enterprise* (Vol. 120). MIT Press.

Craig, J. B., & Moores, K. (2010). Strategically aligning family and business systems using the Balanced Scorecard. *Journal of Family Business Strategy, 1*(2), 78–87.

Kaplan, R. S., & Norton, D. P. (2001). The strategy-focused organization. *Strategy and Leadership, 29*(3), 41–42.

Kaplan, R. S., & Norton, D. P. (2004). *Strategy maps: Converting intangible assets into tangible outcomes*. Harvard Business Press.

Miller, D. (1987). Strategy making and structure: Analysis and implications for performance. *Academy of Management Journal, 30*(1), 7–32.

Miller, D. (1993). The architecture of simplicity. *Academy of Management Review, 18*(1), 116–138.

Miller, D., & Le Breton-Miller, I. (2005). *Managing for the long run: Lessons in competitive advantage from great family businesses*. Harvard Business Press.

Chapter 3: Governance

Breton-Miller, L., & Miller, D. (2006). Why do some family businesses out-compete? Governance, long-term orientations, and sustainable capability. *Entrepreneurship Theory and Practice, 30*(6), 731–746.

Carlock, R., & Ward, J. (2001). *Strategic planning for the family business: Parallel planning to unify the family and business.* Springer.

Fraser, J. (2016). *The handbook of board governance: A comprehensive guide for public, private, and not-for-profit board members.* R. Leblanc (Ed.). John Wiley & Sons.

Garratt, B. (2010). *The fish rots from the head: The crisis in our boardrooms: developing the crucial skills of the competent director.* Profile Books.

Neubauer, F., & Lank, A. G. (2016). *The family business: Its governance for sustainability.* Springer.

Pendergast, J. M., Ward, J. L., & De Pontet, S. B. (2011). *Building a successful family business board: A guide for leaders, directors, and families.* Palgrave Macmillan.

Steier, L. (2001). Family firms, plural forms of governance, and the evolving role of trust. *Family Business Review, 14*(4), 353–368.

Chapter 4: Entrepreneurship

Johnson, B. (1993). Polarity management. *Executive Development, 6,* 28–28.

Johnson, B. (2014). Reflections: A perspective on paradox and its application to modern management. *The Journal of Applied Behavioral Science, 50*(2), 206–212.

Lumpkin, G. T., & Brigham, K. H. (2011). Long-term orientation and intertemporal choice in family firms. *Entrepreneurship Theory and Practice, 35*(6), 1149–1169.

Lumpkin, G. T., Brigham, K., & Moss, T. (2010). Performance of Family Businesses. *Entrepreneurship and Regional Development, 22* (3), 241–264. DOI: 10.1080/08985621003726218

Miller, D. (1992). The Icarus paradox: How exceptional companies bring about their own downfall. *Business Horizons, 35*(1), 24–35.

Schuman, A., Stutz, S., & Ward, J. (2010). *Family business as paradox.* Springer.

Chapter 5: Stewardship

Davis, J. H., Schoorman, F. D., & Donaldson, L. (1997). Toward a stewardship theory of management. *Academy of Management Review, 22*(1), 20–47.

Miller, D., & Le Breton-Miller, I. (2005). Management insights from great and struggling family businesses. *Long Range Planning, 38*(6), 517–530.

Muth, M., & Donaldson, L. (1998). Stewardship theory and board structure: A contingency approach. *Corporate Governance: An International Review, 6*(1), 5–28. DOI: 10.1111/1467-8683.00076

Neubaum, D. O., Dibrell, C., Thomas, C., & Craig, J. B. (2017). Stewardship climate: Scale development and validation. *Family Business Review*, 30 (1), 37–60. DOI: 10.1177/0894486516673701

Chapter 6: Learning Leadership Roles

Adizes, I. (2004). *Managing corporate lifecycles*. The Adizes Institute Publishing.

Lansberg, I. (1999). *Succeeding generations: Realizing the dream of families in business*. Harvard Business Press.

Levinson, H. (1971). Conflicts that plague family businesses. *Harvard Business Review, 49*(2), 90–98.

Moores, K., & Barrett, M. (2003). *Learning family business: Paradoxes and pathways*. (2002) Ashgate Publishing Limited. Reprinted (2010) Bond University Press.

Sonnenfeld, J. A. (1991). *The hero's farewell: What happens when CEOs retire*. Oxford University Press.

Sonnenfeld, J. A., & Spence, P. L. (1989). The parting patriarch of a family firm. *Family Business Review, 2*(4), 355–375.

Chapter 7: The Steward

Ackoff, Russell. (1978). *The art of problem solving: Accompanied by Ackoff's fables,* John Wiley & Sons.

Greenleaf, R. K., & Spears, L. C. (2002). *Servant leadership: A journey into the nature of legitimate power and greatness*. Paulist Press.

Handy, Charles. (1995). *The empty raincoat*. Random House.

Moores, K., & Craig, J. B. (2006). From vision to variables: A scorecard to continue the professionalization of a family firm. In *Handbook of research on family business*, edited by P. Z. Poutziouris, K. X. Smyrnios, and S. B. Klein. Edward Elgar Publisher, in Association with IFERA—The International Family Enterprise Research Academy, pp. 201–202.

Searle, T. P., & Barbuto, J. E. (2011). Servant leadership, hope, and organizational virtuousness: A framework exploring positive micro and macro behaviors and performance impact. *Journal of Leadership & Organizational Studies*, Baker College 2011, 18(1): 107–117.

Spears, L. C. (1995). *Reflections on leadership: How Robert K. Greenleaf's theory of servant-leadership influenced today's top management thinkers* (No. 658.4092 R333r). Wiley.

Chapter 8: The Architect

Bork, D., Jaffe, D., Lane, S., Deshew, L., & Heisler, Q. (1996). *Working with family business*. Jossey-Bass.

Kets de Vries, M. F. R. (1985). The dark side of entrepreneurship. *Harvard Business Review* (November): 160–167, https://hbr.org/1985/11/the-dark-side-of-entrepreneurship

Kets de Vries, M. F. (1991). *Organizations on the couch: Clinical perspectives on organizational behavior and change*. Jossey-Bass.

Lansberg, I. (1983). Managing human resources in family firms: The problem of institutional overlap. *Organizational Dynamics, 12*(1), 39–46.

Sorenson, R. L. (1999). Conflict management strategies used by successful family businesses. *Family Business Review, 12*(4), 325–339.

Chapter 9: The Governor

Craig, J. B., & Moores, K. (2002). How Australia's Dennis Family Corp. professionalized its family business. *Family Business Review, 15*(1), 59–70.

Johannisson, B., & Huse, M. (2000). Recruiting outside board members in the small family business: An ideological challenge. *Entrepreneurship & Regional Development, 12*(4), 353–378.

Lansberg, I. (2007). The tests of a prince. *Harvard Business Review, 85*(9), 92–101.

Ward, J. (2004). "How governing family businesses is different." In *Mastering Global Corporate Governance*, edited by U. Steger, P. Lorange, F. Neubauer, J. Ward, and B. George. England: John Wiley, pp. 135–167.

Chapter 10: The Entrepreneur

Chandler, A. D. (1992). Organizational capabilities and the economic history of the industrial enterprise. *The Journal of Economic Perspectives, 6*(3), 79–100.

Craig, J. B., Cassar, G., & Moores, K. (2006). A 10-year longitudinal investigation of strategy, systems, and environment on innovation in family firms. *Family Business Review, 19*(1), 1–10.

Habbershon, T. G., & Williams, M. L. (1999). A resource-based framework for assessing the strategic advantages of family firms. *Family Business Review, 12*(1), 1–25.

Lai, L. W., & Lorne, F. T. (2014). Transaction cost reduction and innovations for spontaneous cities: Promoting a "meeting" between Coase and Schumpeter. *Planning Theory, 13*(2), 170–188.

Pavitt, K. (1998). Technologies, products and organization in the innovating firm: What Adam Smith tells us and Joseph Schumpeter doesn't. *Industrial and Corporate Change, 7*(3), 433–452.

Shefsky, Lloyd. (2014). *Invent, reinvent, thrive*. McGraw-Hill Publishing.

Zahra, S. A., Hayton, J. C., Neubaum, D. O., Dibrell, C., & Craig, J. (2008). Culture of family commitment and strategic flexibility: The moderating effect of stewardship. *Entrepreneurship Theory and Practice, 32*(6), 1035–1054.

Zawislak, P. A., Cherubini Alves, A., Tello-Gamarra, J., Barbieux, D., & Reichert, F. M. (2012). Innovation capability: From technology development to transaction capability. *Journal of Technology Management & Innovation, 7*(2), 14–27.

Zellweger, T. M., Nason, R. S., & Nordqvist, M. (2012). From longevity of firms to transgenerational entrepreneurship of families introducing family entrepreneurial orientation. *Family Business Review, 25*(2), 136–155.

Index

Note: *illus* denotes White Board Illustration; *t* denotes table.

About the Authors

Justin B. Craig, PhD, is clinical professor of family enterprise and codirector of the Center for Family Enterprises at the Kellogg School of Management, Northwestern University. Before Kellogg, he held faculty positions at Northeastern University in Boston, Bond University in Australia, and Oregon State University. His family business research has been published in leading academic journals. He is a consultant with the Family Business Consulting Group.

Ken Moores, PhD, DBus, is emeritus professor and was the founding director of the Australian Centre for Family Business at Bond University, Australia, where he had previously served as professor of accounting, dean of business, and vice-chancellor and president.